LEAN HARD ON JESUS

Other Crossway books
by Joyce Rogers

Becoming a Woman of Wisdom
The Bible's Seven Secrets to Healthy Eating

LEAN HARD

on

Jesus

God's Great Goodness in Your Darkest Night

JOYCE ROGERS

CROSSWAY BOOKS

A MINISTRY OF
GOOD NEWS PUBLISHERS
WHEATON, ILLINOIS

Lean Hard on Jesus

Copyright © 2005 by Joyce Rogers

Published by Crossway Books
        a ministry of Good News Publishers
        1300 Crescent Street
        Wheaton, Illinois 60187

Cover design: Josh Dennis

Cover photo: Getty Images

Editorial services: Julie-Allyson Ieron, Joy Media

First printing 2005

Printed in the United States of America

All Scripture quotations unless otherwise indicated are taken from the *Holy Bible: New King James Version*. Copyright © 1982 by Thomas Nelson, Inc. Used by permission. All rights reserved.

Scripture quotations marked NIV are taken from the *Holy Bible: New International Version*®. NIV®. Copyright © 1973, 1978, 1984 by International Bible Society. Used by permission of Zondervan Publishing House. All rights reserved. The "NIV" and "New International Version" trademarks are registered in the United States Patent and Trademark Office by International Bible Society. Use of either trademark requires permission of International Bible Society.

Scripture quotations marked KJV taken from the *Holy Bible, King James Version*.

Library of Congress Cataloging-in-Publication Data
Rogers, Joyce
   Lean hard on Jesus : God's great goodness in your darkest night /
Joyce Rogers
     p. cm.
   ISBN 1-58134-674-3 (tpb)
    1. Christian life—Baptist authors. I. Title.
BV4501.3.R66   2005
248.4—dc22
                                  2004017460

BP		14	13	12	11	10	09	08	07	06	05
15	14	13	12	11	10	9	8	7	6	5	4	3	2	1

*Dedicated to precious loved ones who are mentioned in this book.
Together we have learned to lean hard on Jesus.*

*Adrian—my one and only sweetheart
since we were children.
We have walked through some dark valleys together and
have always found our Good Shepherd faithful to bring us through.
Thank you for your loving help and encouragement as I have
labored over this book. Indeed, your life and ministry are so
intertwined with mine that it is impossible to separate them.
I am a better person because of you.*

*Stephen—my firstborn. You were introduced to heartache
when your baby brother, Philip, who had been born on your
fourth birthday, suddenly slipped into heaven. Then recently
you have been faithful to Jesus as you have lived with pain.
God gave you a musical heart, and you have blessed me with this
wonderful gift. I've enjoyed the times you have lived nearby and
miss you greatly now, but I'm grateful for the times we share.
To Cindi and Renae, who have shared and enriched
your life and mine.*

*Gayle—who found comfort after the loss of your first pregnancy
and then great joy in the births of two wonderful sons,
Michael and Adrian. You have brought a lot of love and laughter
into my life. I loved having you live nearby for years and miss you
greatly now. I enjoy having you pop in from time to time.
To Mike, a compassionate and loving man.*

*David—a merciful and tender son who left father, mother,
houses, and land to live out the gospel message in Spain.
That day was one of the happiest, saddest of my life.
To sweet Kelly, "girl of my prayers,"
who shares your love and vision.
To Jonathan, dearly beloved grandson who left his Grammy's arms
when he was just seven months old to live in Spain.
To Stephen, long-awaited niño who arrived just in time for
Thanksgiving and with whom we spent his first Christmas in Spain.*

*I miss you all terribly, but I am so grateful for your faithfulness
to God's call, and I love to come visit as often as I can.
Janice—and her two lovely grown daughters, Angie and Rachel,
who are living testimonies that God works all things together for
good to those who love God. We don't understand the heartaches,
but we rejoice that after the winter, the beauty of spring
has come in your lives and mine. I love having you all near.
Only God can create a beautiful rainbow after the storm.
To Bryan, Andrew, and Breanna—special blessings of
God's goodness and springtime. (Nathan too!)*

*My sweet mama—who shared with me her heart for God.
Although a victim of Alzheimer's, she is with her Savior
and now knows even as she is known.*

*My daddy—a man of character and strength, who passed on to me
his good name. I was his youngest. He called me his "Babe."*

*My brother Curtis—who died of cancer after a valiant fight of faith.
He lived the motto: "Only one life, will soon be past.
Only what's done for Christ will last."*

Contents

Acknowledgments   9

From My Heart   11

Introduction   19

1   Leaning on Jesus in Our Grief   23
    When We Need to Lean the Most

2   "Sonlight" at Midnight   37
    Waiting and Leaning Through the Darkness

3   The Problem of Unanswered Prayer   47
    Keep On Leaning and Keep On Asking

4   Together for Good   61
    Leaning Hard in Times of Disappointment

5   Soul-deep Restoration   71
    From the Hand of the One on Whom We Lean

6   God's Desire for Me   87
    Leaning on Jesus When the Gifts Are Good

7   Choosing to Become Like Jesus   93
    Leaning on Jesus for Direction

8   A Good Land   109
    The Result of Our Leaning on Jesus

9   Sharing His Goodness   123
    Giving Others Someone to Lean Upon

10 Giving Out of Our Weakness   131
    Leaning When We Don't Understand

11 Peace in the Storm   137
    The Ultimate Result of Leaning Hard on Jesus

Epilogue: Have You Heard the Good News?   147
    An Invitation to You to Lean on Jesus

Notes   159

Acknowledgments

Thank you to Lane Dennis and the others at Crossway who have encouraged me in this endeavor and helped bring my dream of helping others to "lean hard on Jesus" to fruition.

And thank you to Julie Ieron, my gifted editor, who caught my vision and helped tie up the loose ends and keep me focused on the main theme of this book. I owe you a great debt of gratitude.

From My Heart

⁓ ⌣

I'm thankful for God's goodness and mercy that have followed me since I was a child. Through His grace they have kept me from many harmful influences.

It has been the purpose of my life to seek the Lord with my whole heart, to love and honor Him and to obey His Word. I invited Jesus to be my Lord when I was nine years old.

The next great love in my life has been Adrian Rogers, my childhood sweetheart from the sixth grade until now. I still have love notes that he dropped by my desk in the sixth grade.

Adrian was saved when he was fourteen years old, the same night as his daddy. I lived across the street from our elementary/junior high school, one block from our church, and two blocks from where Adrian lived. In those years our world consisted of our homes, our school, and our church.

I was standing by his side at a Christian summer assembly in Ridgecrest, N.C., the evening he stepped out during the invitation to surrender his life to Jesus to preach the gospel. There wasn't anyone happier in the whole world than I. At that time, we were too young to be engaged, but deep in my heart I knew that one day I would be Mrs. Adrian Rogers, pastor's wife.

In those teenage years we were leaders in our church youth group. At school he played football, and I was a cheerleader. A picture I gave him back then was signed, "I'll always cheer you on," and I have tried to do just that.

He was called to his first church at Fellsmere, Florida, when he was nineteen years old, at the end of our first year in college. We were married at the beginning of our second year in college. It has been both challenging and fulfilling to be a full-time homemaker and pastor's wife all these years.

We have four wonderful children, who all know our Lord and love and serve Him in their own unique ways. (In addition, our little son Philip ministers from heaven, the highest place of service.) I love being Grammy to nine special grandchildren. Three of my children now live out of town. (One is a missionary in Spain.) I spend a lot of time keeping up with them and praying for them.

I am active in our church where I teach the Children's New Members' Class, sing in the choir, and work in our Women's Ministry, all the while being a support to my husband in all he does.

As this book will reveal, I have known some heartbreaks in my life. As a result, God has given me a heart to reach out to those who are hurting and to share of His sufficiency and goodness in the darkest night. The two greatest truths I have learned are to lean hard on Jesus and to dig deep into His Word.

I never thought I would travel anywhere. But God has enabled Adrian and me to go to many places around the world, ministering His Word. I especially love the land of Israel where we have traveled many times. We have both Arab and Jewish friends whom we love dearly.

I am a normal person. I love to read, write, speak, take pictures, and sing. I am always writing about and drawing lessons from events that have been meaningful to me. Many of them have found their way into the pages of a book. But originally they were written to the Lord or as an expression of what God was speaking to my heart.

I believe with all my heart in the goodness, dependability, and mercy of God. These qualities shine throughout His Word. He has given to me personally the unfailing promise of His goodness and mercy, even in the darkest nights of my soul. And over and over He has proven Himself faithful—to be right there to lean on in times of joy and times of sorrow. I know He is making me more like Jesus and is working all things together for my good. Sometimes I know this from what I see and experience, but always I know it because "the Bible tells me so."

I love His Word. It is the sustaining strength of my life. I long for you to know this magnificent assurance as well. This is why I have opened my heart to share what God has done and is doing in my life.

And what He is doing in my life is sometimes marvelous—and other times painful and trying. We're just coming through one of those trying times.

From Guatemala City to a Hospital Room

It was Monday morning. My clothes were lying on the bed in the guest bedroom just waiting to be packed. Adrian and I were to leave Thursday for Guatemala City in Central America. He was to preach in a citywide Festival for Jesus in a 30,000-seat soccer stadium. The meeting was to be telecast on Saturday across Guatemala and on Sunday by satellite to the entire Spanish-speaking world. This Festival was to be the climax to a five-year partnership of our church with Central American churches. Adrian had preached two similar Festivals in Honduras and Nicaragua.

But instead of packing, I was waiting in a hospital room for the results of my husband's heart catheterization test. Our doctor, Mark Castellaw, had insisted that Adrian get this procedure before he left the country.

Three years earlier Adrian had experienced a minor heart attack in which a stent had been placed in his main artery. The doctor now wanted to be sure everything was still fine. We thought it would be simple. My husband felt fine and was going full steam ahead.

Then Dr. Mark came to tell me that my husband had a serious blockage in his main artery and several lesser blockages. The doctor said Adrian was a "walking time bomb." They needed to do quadruple bypass surgery, and he shouldn't leave the country. In fact, he shouldn't leave the hospital; they would make arrangements for surgery the following morning.

They took me to see Adrian right away and explained everything to the two of us. My husband asked if he couldn't go on to Guatemala and then have the surgery when he returned. All of the consulting physicians said, "Indeed not! It would be too risky."

So the decision was made. It was like a dream—a bad dream.

THE FESTIVAL MUST GO ON

After the first wave of disbelief passed, the first thing to be considered was who would preach at the Festival in Guatemala. Much preparation had been put into this occasion. We had made a trip there several months earlier and met with 2,500 pastors and wives. My husband's picture was on billboards advertising the meetings all over the city.

Our church's influence and backing, my husband's preaching through the television program "*El Amor Que Vale*" (which is dubbed into Spanish), and hundreds of volunteers from our church had together paved the way for the weekend event.

As we prayed about who would preach, only one name surfaced: David Ripley. David is the visionary man whose heart birthed this five-year partnership between Bellevue Church and Central American churches. He is a dynamic preacher of the gospel. Every time he speaks, your heart beats faster for missions outreach.

David was already in Guatemala City preparing for the Festival when he received the call to preach. And preach he did— in the power of the Holy Spirit. Over 7,000 invited Jesus Christ to be their Lord. Only eternity will tell how many in the television audience were changed as well.

Yes, we were disappointed that we couldn't go, but God knew all along and had prepared a man. Wasn't it just like God to allow this young man, who had dreamed this dream, to preach for its fulfillment?

ANOTHER MINISTRY OPPORTUNITY

Meanwhile, back in the hospital God was working. He brought nurses and patients into our path to receive our ministry and our witness.

My husband was privileged to lead a young man, who had been in the hospital awaiting a heart transplant for four months, to the Lord. The man had an artificial heart that he carried around with him. Right in the hospital room he had a spiritual heart transplant when he invited Jesus to come into his life.

Adrian also had the joy of meeting and sharing the love of Christ with a male nurse who was an agnostic. Then there was Traci, a nurse who deeply loved the Lord and at every opportunity came to visit my husband and talk about Jesus.

One day our daughter recalled to her dad and me the story of Philip in Acts 8. God took Philip out of a great revival meeting in

Samaria into the desert to witness to one man—an Ethiopian eunuch—riding in his chariot, reading his Bible. Janice observed, "Daddy, God took you away from the great Festival in Guatemala City to share with a few needy people here in the hospital."

I recounted this story to an African-American minister whose wife was awaiting a heart transplant in the room next to ours. The minister replied, "I was that man." He had heard that my husband was in the room next to his wife and wrote Adrian this note: "Back many years ago in the early 1970s I became a failure in the ministry. I heard you preach on television, and God used you to change my life and restore me to the ministry. You were my school. I learned how to preach by listening to you. I can't believe you're in the next room. Would it be possible for me to come see you?" My husband was privileged to meet him.

Later that evening I took a book my husband had written about Psalm 23 to the room next door and met Brother Roy Goss and his wife, Betty. I visited with them and sang to Betty about the Lord's surrounding presence. Then I prayed and hugged them both and said that when Betty and Adrian were well, we would get together for a meal. I felt an unusual bonding between us.

When I went out in the hall at 7:00 the next morning, the nurse told me Betty had died around 5:00 A.M. I was grief-stricken. Brother Roy had already left the hospital.

We have since spoken and corresponded with Brother Roy several times. Just recently we invited him to spend a Sunday with us. He came to church, and I sat with him on the front row. Adrian told how we had met him and his wife in the hospital and how Betty had gone on to heaven. I had the privilege of giving him a tour around our church while Adrian was preaching in our second morning worship service.

Then we had a delightful time at lunch, talking about the things of the Lord and about what God was leading Brother Roy to do with his life in the future. He thinks that God may want him to begin a recreational center for young people so that they might be reached with the gospel. I think that Betty would be very proud of her husband and of his vision. "Lord, thank You for letting us meet these wonderful Christian friends, and please fulfill this man's dream."

We didn't understand at first why God prevented us from going to Guatemala City for that tremendous Festival. But He had everything under control, and He knew He had made an appointment with Roy and Betty Goss on a crucial day for them.

LESSONS IN LEANING

Many months have passed since my husband's bypass surgery. He has experienced constant monitoring, numerous pills, lack of appetite, low energy, sleepy spells, forgetfulness, and a heart flutter (to mention just a few). Gradually, most of these have diminished or completely gone away. After six weeks Adrian was able to attend the graduations of two special granddaughters. He has been able to pick up his responsibilities a little at a time. His first Sunday back in the pulpit was July 4, and what a celebration that was!

Even though these have been trying days, I must say we have experienced some sweet times. Adrian has been a thoughtful and appreciative patient. We have spent a lot of time together. We have read God's Word and prayed together. God has brought peace and contentment in the midst of this storm.

We have discovered anew the value of friends and loved ones. They have bombarded heaven with prayers on our behalf—prayers God was gracious to answer in the affirmative. These friends have showered us with acts of kindness, delicious meals, flowers, and cards.

We would not have asked for this trial, but we would not trade the lessons learned nor the love given and received. Waiting on God and learning a new level of patience have been key lessons during these months of recovery.

Most of all, we have experienced (not for the first time in our lives) the great strength that comes from "leaning hard on Jesus." We dug deep into His wonderful Word and discovered fresh and fitting promises. One that I claimed is found in Psalm 31:24: "Be of good courage, and He shall strengthen your heart, all you who hope in the Lord."

Because I am a "musical person," God also speaks to me through music. I don't play the piano well, but I have a collection of simple praise worship songbooks. I go though them and discover new songs, "dog ear" them, and sing and play them over and over again to the Lord. During these months of recovery God has given me numerous new songs to sing to Him, alongside beloved old ones. One of my favorite new songs is titled, "He Is Able." The message of this song is that He is able to accomplish whatever concerns me today. I can testify to this wonderful truth: With God nothing is impossible.

Thank you, Lord, for allowing me to lean hard on You and to draw strength from the many precious promises in Your wonderful Word.

Introduction

After reading about my most recent lesson in leaning on Jesus in the previous "From My Heart" section, you may be wondering a bit about the title of this book. You may be asking, When do we lean hard on Jesus?

In times of trouble, like when a spouse or child is gravely ill? Certainly then.

In times of national tragedy, like September 11? Yes, then we lean hard on Him.

In times of personal grief or pain? Most definitely we lean hard on Jesus then. Really hard.

But that is only part of the answer. For when we catch a glimpse of who we are in light of who He is, when we see rightly our utter dependence and need for Him, we will naturally lean hard on Jesus—in times when we see things working together for good and times when we don't see anything but the darkest night.

It takes courage, and it takes faith to lean on Him. For leaning assumes that Someone will be there, willing and able to catch us. Let me assure you, my friend, in case you are wondering—He'll be there for you, as He has been for me. I know this because His character is unchanging—He IS good.

WHY WE CAN LEAN ON JESUS

There is one answer and only one to the question of why we can be assured that if we lean on Jesus, He'll be there for us: God is good. All the time.

I asked myself this question: How and when did I learn of the goodness of God? I could not remember. There was no day or hour. It seems I've always believed in His goodness. But, no, I had to have learned it somewhere, from someone, sometime. Or was it many places, many people, many times?

Was it a hymn I sang? My mother's whispered assurance in a dark night? When I memorized Psalm 23 as a child? Did I learn it from a sermon I heard preached or from the lips of a Sunday school teacher? Did I perceive His goodness when I gazed upon a glorious sunset or watched a multicolored rainbow make its appearance after the rain? I'm sure it must have been "here a little, there a little" (Isa. 28:10).

When did I receive the magnificent assurance that "all things" (the so-called good and the so-called bad) would "work together for good to those who love God, to those who are the called according to His purpose" (Rom. 8:28)? Indeed, I can't remember. But in the darkest night and in the starkest tragedies, these words ring out with jubilant hope. As surely as I live, I believe His promise. Deep within my soul I possess this assurance.

How grateful I am that I've never doubted His goodness. This assurance has followed me from the mountaintop to the darkest of valleys. I knew He was there and that He was good—all the time. In fact, in the dark valleys I learned new depths of His goodness.

I realize now that as a child I had a shallow understanding of His goodness. But it was a beginning. I have walked through dark places. I have looked into the black abyss of circumstances beyond my control. He has taught me that His goodness is much more profound than I had ever dreamed.

The goodness of God is one of the great themes that runs throughout the Bible. I have read the Bible through, focusing on this subject. It has become an exciting treasure hunt, searching for His goodness. Now I have become so programmed to recognize His goodness that it jumps off the page when I read.

We are encouraged in Psalm 34:8 to "taste and see that the LORD is good." God is "oh, so good!" We need to learn to recognize God's goodness in everyday living. His goodness surrounds us on every hand.

Will you join me now in this treasure hunt to discover for yourself His great goodness? You will find that truly there will never be a time in your life when the goodness of God won't have Him at your side, if only you'll have the faith to lean hard on Him.

1

Leaning on Jesus in Our Grief

When We Need to Lean the Most

∼ ∽

I had been discussing the tragic circumstances of the Holocaust with an acquaintance. He told me he respected all religions but that he himself wasn't religious. He had not been raised to believe in God. He was not an atheist now, but he could not reconcile tragic circumstances with the concept of a good God.

Our conversation went something like this:

"Why did God let these horrible things happen?"

"Just ask Him, my friend; and He will show you the truth about who He is."

"No, He won't show me. Why did He let those horrible things happen? He won't show me."

This is one of the great underlying problems in all of life. Through the centuries, philosophers have raised questions related to "horrible things" and the goodness of God. Here are some of the questions posed:

◇ If God knows, and He doesn't care, how could He be good?

◇ If God cares, but He doesn't know, how could He be omniscient?

◇ If He knows and cares, but He is helpless to do anything, how could He be omnipotent?

◇ If He knows, cares, and is doing something about it, that is a magnificent assurance we can depend upon.

This magnificent assurance is what this book is all about. Learn this, and it will bring great hope even in the darkest night. As we begin our journey into leaning on Jesus, allow me to share with you some of the answers to the "why" questions I wanted to communicate with my friend.

WHY GOD ALLOWS "THESE HORRIBLE THINGS"

As I have pondered these questions for many years, I have pragmatically arrived at the following five answers:

1. *To show the sinfulness of man without God.*

Most people will acknowledge that "no one is perfect." We easily excuse ourselves for our so-called mistakes, inconsistencies, and faults. These things we freely acknowledge to be annoying and frustrating. But when it comes to admitting our sinfulness, it is a different story. We humans as a race find it demeaning to confess that we are totally depraved—capable of the lowest, despicable deed—unless we are faced head-on with that truth.

Nevertheless, if left to himself, without the redeeming power of God, man will invent the vilest crimes against his fellowman. Then when mankind sinks to its lowest miserable state, people want to blame God for allowing it.

However, terrible outbursts of wickedness like the Holocaust, Pearl Harbor, the modern slaughter of the innocents (the Abortion Holocaust), and the horror of September 11, 2001, reveal what all people are capable of when left to work out their own goodness without God. Sometimes it takes coming face to face with tragedy to make us vulnerable enough to be willing to face the truth about ourselves and our sinful state.

2. *To bring judgment on man's sin and call us back to God.*

When man's awful sinfulness is revealed, God reveals His absolute righteousness. The contrast is blinding. God demands judgment on a perverse people. Judgment awakens these same people to their need of Someone more powerful than they to lift them from such depths of degradation.

Sinful man therefore is called back to his need of a relationship with a holy God and the realization that without a transformation he cannot have this relationship with such a good and righteous God.

3. *To reveal God's sufficiency to us and to others.*

When God's judgment descends upon us and we feel the crushing consequences of a life lived in defiance of Him, we run to Him as our only hope for deliverance. After all, if we don't turn to Him, where shall we turn in life's darkest hour?

I love the passage in John 6 where Jesus asks His disciples if they want to desert Him in rough times, and Peter answers for the disciples: "Lord, to whom shall we go? You have the words of eternal life." In times like these, where else can we go but to His side?

As we reach out to Him in utter despair, He reveals His sufficiency. Through brokenness we experience a dependence upon our great God and a deeper fellowship with Him. This experience creates a wholeness in our lives we'll never know without Him.

The ultimate blessing is that such a transformation takes place that we become a channel through which God's sufficiency is revealed to those around us. This transformation in our lives permeates our entire being with light, because we are now constantly exposed to Jesus Christ, who is the Light. Our lives also are saturated with truth, because we are constantly exposed to Jesus Christ, who is the Truth.

4. *To show us the true priorities of life.*

With the One who is both Light and Truth as our constant companion and teacher, we begin to see clearly the true priorities in life. The motto for our church reveals this insight: "O send out thy light and thy truth" (Ps. 43:3 KJV). We can then see the vanity of all that the world seeks without God.

We realize the truth that fame and fortune are meaningless without Him. These are only servants to be used to show others the One who brings true identity and riches. We see worldly pleasure for what it is: empty and unsatisfying. True pleasure only results from a relationship with the One who satisfies the soul—Jesus Christ.

We see earthly possessions as only a cheap substitute for the possession of eternal life through the matchless Savior. Through times of trial God teaches us that only when we master these things can they become meaningful servants to be used to bring glory to Him.

5. *To perfect us, testing and making us into His likeness.*

God is constantly calling sinners to Himself. We could probably understand more readily how bad things happen to bad people as a judgment on their sins and as a means to draw them to God.

But the Bible says, "the goodness of God leads you to repentance" (Rom. 2:4). So we see that good things sometimes happen to bad people. And if that isn't difficult enough to understand, we are faced with the dilemma that bad things often happen to good people.

Why? Job expressed it well: "When He has tested me, I shall come forth as gold" (Job 23:10). He follows that statement with another, in verse 16: "For God made my heart weak, and the Almighty terrifies me."

Job did not know the answer to the hard question, "Why?" And even when I am privy to the reason God let Satan destroy practically everything Job possessed, frankly my heart is not satisfied. Oh, yes, there are reasons. There are answers to the question, "Why?" I have shared with you some of the potential answers to that haunting question. But when heartache and tragedy have knocked at my heart's door, none of these reasons has satisfied my broken heart.

WHEN ANSWERS AREN'T ENOUGH

However, when in desperation I have sought Him and Him alone, I have been satisfied. If, indeed, you knew the particular answer to your dilemma, that answer could not heal your broken heart or satisfy your longing soul. Only Jesus can satisfy your soul. I love the song that expresses this so wonderfully: "When answers aren't enough, there is Jesus."

Then when you are satisfied with Him, He may or may not answer your questions. But if you are questioning His goodness, He will never give you understanding or satisfaction. It would be impossible if your heart is filled with bitterness toward Him.

THE GREAT CLASSIC ON GOOD AND EVIL

Perhaps there are no sufficient answers to the haunting questions that arise when we stare into the face of the awful and sometimes sinister tragedies of life. But the main issue that we must resolve is: "Do we believe in the ultimate goodness of God?" Can we say with Job, "Though He slay me, yet will I trust Him" (Job 13:15)? Do we know that all things work together for good if we love God and want to do His will?

If we are to know, if we are to have the kind of faith that will hold in the darkest hour of our life, we must be convinced of the goodness of God.

Of course, the great classic on good and evil and why even good people suffer is the book of Job. In my darkest hours of tragedy I have found hope within the pages of this book. When my baby died, one of the first verses that came to me was Job 1:21: "The LORD gave and the LORD has taken away; Blessed be the name of the LORD." These words of one who had "been there" helped me to praise the Lord in the face of inexplicable tragedy. I, too, have joined with Job in his classic affirmation of faith in God: "Though He slay me, yet will I trust Him" (Job 13:15).

THE RISK OF CHOICES

Enter the conflict between good and evil. Why did God allow evil? Why did He make us so we could choose wrong and sin against Him? Isn't that the essence of all our grief and problems?

I think it is most simply illustrated by a visual aid I use in my children's class for new Christians. I purchased a battery-operated robot. All of the children are fascinated by this little toy. The robot only does two things—the things he is programmed to do. He is programmed to walk and to shoot some harmless darts if you push the right buttons. He is a neat toy, but he isn't worth what I paid for him except for the lesson he helps me teach. I always ask the children, "What important things can a robot not do?" Their answers vary: A robot can't love and be loved. It can't give a hug— or receive one. It can't make a friend. It can't know and be known.

It can't make choices. It can only do the things its creator made it to do—walk and shoot darts.

God took the terrible risk of making man and woman with the ability to choose between right and wrong. If they could not choose, then love and good would be meaningless. Human beings would be no more than the battery-operated robot, programmed to do one thing with no choice and no ability to know and be known.

When God made Adam and Eve and all the world, He said, "it was very good" (Gen. 1:31). But then He dared to give them a choice. He put the tree of the knowledge of good and evil in the middle of the garden and said, ". . . of the tree of the knowledge of good and evil you shall not eat, for in the day that you eat of it you shall surely die" (Gen. 2:17).

Now why would a good God, who saw everything that He created as very good, say that they could not eat of the fruit of that tree? Because it was good for them to have the possibility of making a choice. But even to have that possibility meant that there had to be the possibility of making a wrong choice. Otherwise, they would have been just like robots that could not experience love nor a meaningful relationship with God. What a toylike, meaningless existence that would have been.

THE CAPACITY FOR EVIL

I do understand that the possibility for making a wrong choice created the capacity for evil. But even Satan was originally a good creation. He was Lucifer, son of the morning. He likewise was given a choice, and He chose to rebel. He wanted to overthrow God and sit on His throne—to be like the Most High. And he continues to rebel against the Almighty and His creation on earth (Isa. 14:12-15).

We can choose to follow Satan and try to become our own little tin gods, or we can choose to allow Jesus Christ to sit on the throne of our lives and allow Him to be Lord. Will we choose to rebel or in meekness bow before Him? Will we follow His example—the King of Kings and Lord of Lords who humbled Himself and became like a servant? Will we choose good instead of evil? Then we must choose Jesus, for only He is good, because He is God.

GOD'S PROVISION FOR SINFUL MAN

God knew people would sin by making wrong choices, causing separation from Himself. Nevertheless, this good God had already made provision for sinful people before they actually sinned. In God's mind Jesus was "slain from the foundation of the world" (Rev. 13:8).

No, I don't understand it all. I frankly don't believe we have the capacity in our finite existence to understand completely. However, this doesn't mean that we shouldn't study and seek all the understanding we can gain on this subject.

OUR ONLY GUARANTEE—GOD

When priceless possessions and precious people are taken away from us, most of us usually focus on these lost things. I think back thirty years ago. I went to visit the mother of a child in my Sunday school class. As we talked, I realized she had lost a baby about the same time as I had. At that time it had been about fifteen years. Yet she had held a bitterness toward God all those years. Although God had given her two more children, she was still miserable. She had never found God in all her pain.

I, too, had known the sharpness of the "sting of death." I still don't know the answer to the question, "Why?" But I searched for God amidst my pain, and I found Him. He was not hard to find when I took the time to look. He was there waiting for me in the darkness.

In his book *Three Philosophies of Life,* Peter Kreeft says about Job, "The thing he keeps talking about is not his sores or his lost possessions or even his lost family but rather his lost God. He felt God-forsaken; apparently he thought that he would never see God's face. That is the thing he longed for most, even if it meant death."[1] Job cried out, "Oh, that I knew where I might find Him" (Job 23:3). That can be our cry as well.

In our nation we have assumed that we are all guaranteed life, liberty, and the pursuit of happiness. Of course, these are all things we would each want; but Mr. Kreeft is absolutely right when he states, "Only one thing in life is guaranteed. Not happiness, not the pursuit of happiness, not liberty, not even life. The only thing we are absolutely guaranteed is the only thing we absolutely need in conforming our wants to reality—God."[2]

BROKEN HEDGES

During the devastating flooding of the mighty Mississippi and Miramac Rivers in 1993, I flew over the flooded area surrounding St. Louis, Missouri. It was sad and awesome to behold from the air. The effects were so far reaching that the flood got the attention of the whole nation. It made the headlines of my local newspaper way over in Memphis, Tennessee.

Someone told me that in the outlying area, only one church was not flooded. Thousands were homeless. People experienced billions of dollars of damage to their property. *Why, oh why, did God let this happen?* Many good, innocent people were affected as well as the wicked. Could this be part of God's judgment on America?

The Bible teaches that God builds hedges around individuals and nations, protecting them from Satan's destruction. God allowed the hedge around Job's life to be temporarily taken down to test Job (Job 1:9-12). Likewise, the psalmist asks God, "Why have You broken down her hedges, so that all who pass by the way pluck her fruit?" (Ps. 80:12).

In Isaiah 5:5-6 Israel is pictured as God's vineyard. We read that God took the protective hedge down around this nation because of its sin. Then Satan could come in and wreak havoc. We have an example of this in the book of Amos. God said, "'In the day I punish Israel for their transgressions, I will also visit destruction on the altars of Bethel; and the horns of the altar shall be cut off and fall to the ground. I will destroy the winter house along with the summer house; the houses of ivory shall perish, and the great houses shall have an end,' says the Lord" (Amos 3:14-15).

Yes, it was God who sent famine; it was God who sent drought; it was God who sent blight and mildew and pestilence. He sent these catastrophes as a warning, but the people of that day would not seek God. "'Yet you have not returned to Me,' says the Lord" (Amos 4:10). God was longsuffering, but His patience finally ran out. Amos quotes God as saying, "'Therefore thus will I do to you, O Israel; because I will do this to you, prepare to meet your God, O Israel!'" (Amos 4:12).

What Amos is telling the people is this: Because you didn't know Him, because you didn't even seek to know Him when He sent judgment in various forms—get ready—for you are going to meet Him. Not in the manner in which you'd like, I'm sure. In essence his message said, "If you haven't met Him before, let me introduce you to God. The Lord, the God of Hosts, is His name."

"For behold, He who forms mountains, and creates the wind, who declares to man what His thought is, and makes the morning darkness, who treads the high places of the earth—The Lord God of hosts is His name" (Amos 4:13).

LET ME INTRODUCE YOU TO GOD

When disaster comes, we are to examine our lives and seek God. We may or may not be the direct cause of the trouble. We live in a world cursed by sin. All of us will suffer more or less the consequences of sin—our own personal sin or the sin of others.

Three times in the fifth chapter of Amos the Israelites are admonished to seek the Lord.

> *"For thus says the LORD to the house of Israel, 'Seek Me and live.'" (v. 4)*

> *"Seek the LORD and live, lest He break out like fire in the house of Joseph, and devour it, with no one to quench it in Bethel." (v. 6)*

> *"Seek good and not evil, that you may live; so the LORD God of hosts will be with you, as you have spoken." (v. 14)*

Therefore it follows that we are to "Hate evil, love good; establish justice in the gate. It may be that the LORD God of hosts will be gracious to the remnant of Joseph" (v. 15).

For those of us in the United States who are seeking God, it will be obvious to us that our country as a whole has forsaken Him. The openly flaunted immorality, the rebellion against authority, the killing of the unborn, and seeking sanction for the perverted homosexual lifestyle are all evidences of this departure.

I believe that national, wide-scale natural disasters have begun to escalate. As a prelude in 1992, we saw the devastation of Hurricane Andrew in southeast Florida. Then in summer 1993 the widespread flooding along the Mississippi River; then the horrible consequences of the earthquake in Los Angeles in 1993. A number of tornadoes swept across the mid-south in 1999. One in Oklahoma was a mile wide, lasting for hours and destroying many homes.

Then came September 11, 2001. This was the greatest man-made tragedy to happen to the United States. I'll never forget that day. Our granddaughter Renae called from Florida. All she said was, "Turn on the television. A plane has crashed into one of the Twin Towers in New York."

Then we stared in unbelief as we saw another plane hit the other tower. Almost numb with horror, we watched those beautiful, gigantic buildings implode. Only two months before, Adrian and I had stood on the top of one of the towers with our granddaughter Rachel and looked out over New York City. Then we had looked straight up from the bottom to the top of the towering giants and marveled at their magnificence.

Now people were frantically running away from them, screaming. It seemed like a nightmare, but indeed it was real. Our eyes stayed glued to this awful tragedy being played out before us. Then news broke of another plane crashing into the Pentagon, then another crashing in a field in Pennsylvania. We wondered where it would stop. Wholesale terrorism had invaded our shores. We paused to pray, "Oh, God, oh, God, help us. Help these horrified victims. Oh, God, help our country."

Then it hit me: "Where are David, Kelly, and the boys?" They are missionaries to Spain, and just hours before they had boarded a flight returning to that country from their stateside assignment. I ran to call Kelly's Mom, Pat, and we concluded by the schedule that they were in the air—somewhere between Amsterdam and Madrid. We fervently prayed for their safe arrival.

Pat called a fellow missionary and asked him to put a note on David and Kelly's door, telling them to call home as soon as they arrived. Around midnight we received a call. They were safe. They had not heard a word about the attack until they read the note. How grateful we were.

Then my husband called our church and set up a prayer meeting. Around noon people began to pour in and pack our 7,000-seat worship center. We had all come to seek God. He was our only hope.

I rarely turn on the television in the daytime, but for weeks I turned it on when I got up in the morning to see if some other horrible thing had happened. I left it playing in the background all day so that when I passed it, I could catch a glimpse of the news.

Finally I decided that only occasionally would I check the news. I needed to be more focused on the Lord. I searched and decided to study Psalm 46. I memorized and meditated on those familiar words for weeks: "God is our refuge and strength, a very present help in trouble. Therefore we will not fear, even though the earth be removed, and though the mountains be carried into the midst of the sea" (vv. 1-2).

Indeed, our whole lives have been changed since that horrible day. I hope they have been changed for the better—to shake us from our lethargy into seeking the Lord with our whole hearts.

RETURN BEFORE IT IS TOO LATE

Has God removed the protective hedge from America? Is He issuing a loving call to return before it is too late? Is this a part of God's thorns and thistles for man's sake? Some have been offended at this thought. Yet if He allowed our nation to continue on in its perversion and greedy lifestyle, would He be a good God? Each of us must ponder these possibilities and seek the Lord, not only on our own behalf but for our nation as a whole.

Is it too late? Will everyone have to repent before God is gracious? Oh, that everyone would turn from their sins like those in the city of Nineveh who repented in sackcloth and ashes, from the greatest to the lowest. But "It may be that the LORD God of hosts will be gracious to the remnant" (Amos 5:15). Will *you* be a part of that remnant who will seek the Lord and live?

It is so easy for us to look around and see the awful sins people have committed against each other, the disasters of nature and of man. But will we look around and find the good, the gracious benefits that God has continued to pour out on us? Will we seek God when judgment comes in disaster? Will we run to Him and lean on Him when His goodness is displayed in blessings? Will we return and love God? Then we will *know* that "all things work together for good."

PRACTICING THE PROMISES

Lord, I WILL . . .

◇ Examine my life and turn from any known sins.

◇ Memorize Psalm 46 and meditate on Jesus as my refuge and strength in time of trouble.

◇ Turn to God's Word when tragic events occur.

◇ Search the Bible for stories of believers who went through tragedy and came out on the other side with a stronger faith.

◇ Repeat along with Job, "Though He slay me, yet will I trust Him" (Job 13:15)—and determine to live it out.

2

"Sonlight" at Midnight

Waiting and Leaning
Through the Darkness

Although it has been more than forty years, I can still remember the day God enrolled me in the beginning class, "Times of Darkness 101." It was a lovely Mother's Day afternoon, and I was going to take a nap. Before lying down, I decided to check on the baby in the crib.

Baby Philip looked so strange. Frightened, I shouted for my husband. "Adrian! Come quickly!" Horror stricken, I asked, "Is he dead?"

Our older children, ages four and two, were taking their naps. Adrian placed Philip's little body inside his coat and drove as quickly as he could to the hospital. While he was gone, I prayed aloud those familiar words from Psalm 23 I had learned as a child: "The LORD is my shepherd; I shall not want. . . . Yea, though I walk through the valley of the shadow of death, I will fear no evil; for You are with me. Your rod and Your staff, they comfort me. . . ."

It seemed like an eternity before Adrian returned, although it was only a short while. I knew from the look on his face as he came up the sidewalk that our precious baby Philip was now in the arms of Jesus. The words *sudden crib death* (now known as SIDS) took on an all-too personal dimension.

Prior to that moment, we had never lost a loved one. I remember feeling dark, oh so dark, as we embraced each other. We had comforted others. Now it was we who desperately needed comfort. Adrian and I made a few phone calls to family and friends. Soon they began to arrive, offering their love and sympathy.

Philip's funeral was held in our hometown sixty miles away. As we were leaving our house, the windows of our church next door were open, and we could hear the people singing, "No, never alone; no never alone. He promised never to leave me. Never to leave me alone."[1] Although the darkness was never deeper, God's presence was never so real. What heretofore had been an easily sung gospel song became a promise and a reality that I clung to with all my might: "He promised never to leave me. Never to leave me alone."

Even so, time after time torrents of grief would engulf me. Sometimes I literally held my hands up to God and said, "Lord, here, take my broken heart. It is too much for me to bear."

I learned two life-changing lessons in those days. As I mentioned in the Introduction to this book, I have called them, "Lean Hard," and "Dig Deep." First, I began to learn how to lean on Jesus.

Someone sent me the following poem. In the ensuing years I have given many copies away. I memorized the words in those days. I treasure the message still.

Lean Hard

Child of My love, lean hard,
And let Me feel the pressure of thy care;

I know thy burden, child, I shaped it;
Poised it in Mine own hand, made no proportion
In its weight to thine unaided strength;

For even as I laid it on, I said,
I shall be near, and while he leans on Me,
This burden shall be Mine, not his;
So shall I keep My child within the circling arms
of My own love.

Here lay it down, nor fear
To impose it on a shoulder which upholds
The government of worlds. Yet closer come;
Thou art not near enough; I would embrace thy care
So I might feel My child reposing on My breast.

Thou lovest Me? I knew it. Doubt not then
But loving Me, lean hard.
—AUTHOR UNKNOWN

The second of those lessons was digging deep into His Word. I had loved and believed God's Word since I was a little girl, but for this piercing pain, I had to dig deeper.

He began to direct me to verses about praising at all times. I discovered Psalm 63:3-4 (KJV), which became my life verses: "Because thy lovingkindness is better than life, my lips shall praise thee. Thus will I bless thee while I live: I will lift up my hands in thy name."

Psalm 34:1 was another blessing in those days: "I will bless the LORD at all times; His praise shall continually be in my mouth." A third passage the Lord brought to mind was one we mentioned briefly in the previous chapter from Job 1:21: "The LORD gave, and the LORD has taken away; blessed be the name of the LORD."

I did not *feel* like praising God, and I did not want to offer fake praise to God. That would produce no more than a sick grin. God showed me that He wanted me to *faith* my praise to Him. How I thank Him that it works. He also taught me just to glance at my circumstances but to *gaze* upon Jesus. During this period of learning and waiting, He became my focus. I came to know Him in a way I never had before. In the words of Roy Hession, I learned that "it is enough to see Jesus and to go on seeing Him."

The waiting and leaning involved giving up my right to understand why. Through the strength of God's Holy Spirit and inspired by a Spirit-filled gospel song by Ira Stanphill, "We'll Talk It Over," I handed *my right to understand why* over to God and found myself inexplicably content to wait for reasons 'til after a while.

Then in a practical way, God taught me to do what lay at hand: fold the diapers, sweep the floor, visit the sick, cook the meals, sing a song, study His Word. Day by day He took me by the hand and led me out of darkness into His marvelous light.

Times of Darkness 401

Fast-forward forty years to the moment God enrolled me in an advanced course in His school of Christian living. I call it "Times of Darkness 401." In fact, it was the most difficult class in Christian living I had ever experienced. If I didn't want to fail, I needed all the help I could get.

It is not necessary to give the details. I will just say that it involved a devastating circumstance in the lives of precious loved ones. I can testify that the experience, humanly speaking, was like the blackness of midnight.

When my baby died, I knew I could either cast myself completely on God or turn away from Him. At that time I found Him to be more than sufficient for my need. But this latest hour of darkness was worse than death. I asked a thousand whys, trying to figure it all out. But I was exhausted at the end of many a day, knowing that only God held the answer.

Now I can tell you I'm grateful for the lessons I learned in "Times of Darkness 101." They helped me endure this latest struggle. I cast myself on my God over and over again. I knew what it was to lean hard on Him, but once again I struggled—more vigorously this time—with giving up my *right to understand why.* Somehow it was easier to do when Philip died.

Oh, I praised Him; and when I did, He brought peace. And when I praised Him, I cannot describe the peace He brought in the midst of even this storm. His joy flooded my soul when my eyes were filled with tears.

LIFE IS LIKE A RACE

In the race of life sometimes the running is easy, sometimes hard. At times we fall and struggle to get up. It seems that all our strength is gone.

But never forget those in the *heavenly grandstand* cheering us on. And never lose sight of the goal and the crown to be won. But most of all, look forward to our Savior's, "Well done, my child, well done." Here is the testimony of my precious loved one.

The Heavenly Grandstand

I was running the race of life, and the wind was at my back;
There was never a fairer day to run, never a smoother track.
So with my head held high as the miles raced by,
I ran with careless ease.
I would run this race, I would win first place
so my Master I would please.

Then an unforeseen hand rudely pushed me down,
And I fell with a thud to the cold, cruel ground;
And broken and bruised, I began to cry
As the other runners all passed me by.
"Lord, help me please! I can't run any more;
I'm broken and battered, I'm tired and sore;
I don't think I can make it, I just want to die,
I don't even have what it takes to try."

And as I lay bleeding upon the ground,
A vast "cloud of witnesses" gathered round.
They were heroes of old, all the saints of the ages,
Who through weakness were strong
And through faith made courageous.
They started to cheer and to wildly applaud,
And their voices rose up giving glory to God.
And then to myself I said, "How can this be?"
For the saints of the ages were cheering for me!
Then Abel cried out, "There is power in the blood!"
And Noah said, "He'll keep you safe through the flood."
Then Jacob said, "Weary one, lean on the Lord,"
And Moses cried out, "Child, look to the reward!"
Then Sarah stepped forward, holding Abraham's hand,
And they both said, "Trust God when you don't understand."
In God's promises, child, you must always believe,
For sometimes He'll do things you just can't conceive.
Come on! You can do it! Get up off your face
And run with endurance the rest of the race.
And remember, my child, when your strength is all gone,
The saints of the ages are cheering you on!"

So I rose to my feet midst their thunderous ovation
And started to run with great determination;
And that's when I saw Him, my Savior and Lord,
And I knew in my heart I must win the reward
To cast down before Him the crown that I'd won,
And to hear Him say to me, "Well done, child, well done!"
JANICE ROGERS EDMISTON

LESSONS IN THE WAITING ROOM

In this crisis of the 401 class, just as in the crisis of my husband's heart surgery, I felt so helpless—so powerless. I thought, *If there were only something I could do.* But I had to find contentment in waiting on God.

Why does God take longer than we want Him to? He wants us to look to Him, to get to know Him better, to desire the Giver more than the gift. He also desires to develop in us patience and endurance. I have discovered how impatient I am, how much I want an answer—right now.

Andrew Murray wrote,

> If anyone is inclined to lose hope, because he does not have such patience, be encouraged. It is in the process of our weak and very imperfect waiting that God Himself by His hidden power strengthens us and works out in us the patience of the saints, the patience of Christ Himself. And if you sometimes feel as if patience is not your gift, then remember, it is God's gift.
>
> In waiting on God it is important that we submit not because we are forced to; but because we lovingly and joyfully consent to be in the hands of our blessed Father. Patience then becomes our highest blessing; and our highest grace. It honors God and gives Him time to have His way with us. It is the highest expression of our faith in His goodness and faithfulness. True patience is the losing of our self-will in His perfect will.[2]

In recent months my attention has been drawn to how many times we are called upon to wait. I have waited at the red light and the stop sign. I have waited at the doctor's office and in the hospital. There is even a room in some places called the waiting room. I wait for my husband to come home for dinner, for my grown children to come for the holidays. I wait for the clerk in the department store. I wait in line at the bank. In fact, much of my life is spent waiting.

I have also learned that if I wait on others very long, I get impatient. What will I do while I am waiting? I had never even thought about it before, but over the years I have developed a plan—things to keep me occupied and fill my waiting moments.

Recently God brought to mind that the thing I did the least while I was waiting on others was to pray. This was vividly brought to my attention when I found myself in one of the examining rooms at my doctor's office. I had forgotten to bring my Bible or a book. There was not even a magazine to read or paper on which to write a letter. I thought, *What a predicament. What a waste of precious time.*

It was at that moment when I heard the inward rebuke: *You can always pray. You do not need pen or paper. You do not need a book or even the Bible to make contact with Me. Isolated from everyone, sitting on this examining table, you can have fellowship with Me—the source of all your needs. I am at the red light, under the dryer in the beauty parlor, in the waiting room at the hospital—yes, in the doctor's examination room. It does not have to be a waste of time as you are waiting on circumstances or waiting on others. If you could only recognize these times as opportunities to wait on Me, it would revolutionize your life.*

It is in times of waiting, whether planned or unplanned, that we come to recognize who God is—the One we are waiting for. He is a good God, filled with mercy and judgment. He has all power and wisdom. He is the source of our love and joy and peace. We must be still and wait to know His presence.

Andrew Murray wrote, "Seek not only the help or the gift, seek Him; wait for Him. Give God the glory by resting in Him, by trusting Him fully, by waiting patiently for Him. This patience honors Him greatly; it leaves Him as God on the throne to do His work; it yields self wholly into His hands. It lets God be God."[3]

I am just beginning to remember this truth—waiting on others can remind us to wait on Him. Instead of becoming impatient, I find myself looking forward to those times. In times of waiting I love to search His Word. Psalm 18 is my favorite chapter to meditate upon during those moments.

A PRAYER FOR WAITING MOMENTS

Deliverance seldom comes in the way I expect it to, but as I waited in my times of advanced testing, I prayed in the words of this psalm-style poem:

> *"My God,*
> *I will love You.*
> *You are my strength,*
> *My rock,*
> *My fortress;*
> *You are my high tower.*
>
> *Oh, my God,*
> *I run into You to hide.*
> *Oh, God, it is so dark*
> *I cannot see.*
>
> *Please hold my hand*
> *and lead me through*
> *this darkness.*
>
> *Take my hand.*
> *We can run through the troop*
> *and leap over this wall.*
>
> *Hallelujah! Hallelujah!*

Often there is nothing I can do but wait on God and say, "Thank You for 'Sonlight' at Midnight."

PRACTICING THE PROMISES

Lord, I WILL . . .

◇ Turn to Jesus and seek Him with my whole heart when bad things happen.

◇ Search the Scriptures for encouragement and strength when I don't think I can carry on.

◇ Remember and thank God for the cloud of witnesses cheering me on.

◇ Learn to pray while waiting on God in unexplainable circumstances.

◇ Write an affirmation of my choice to lean on Jesus—in the form of prose or poetry or even song.

3

The Problem of Unanswered Prayer

Keep On Leaning and Keep On Asking

~ ~

The greatest lesson I've learned and am learning about leaning on Jesus is to pray and keeping on praying to God in times of darkness. I have no doubt that God will answer our prayers—even our prayers in the difficult situation I described in the last chapter. I just don't always know when and how His answer will come.

And it is this waiting for answered prayer that makes leaning on Jesus so much more difficult to do. It would be easy to run to Him, lean on Him, ask of Him, and see an immediate answer. Oh, how quickly I would run to Him if He worked in that way. Occasionally, He does. But *only* occasionally. Mostly His first answer to my prayers is "Keep waiting on Me. Keep leaning on Me. Keep trusting Me when you don't think I'm working. Don't worry. I am working. Just wait."

THE GREATEST LESSON

The invitation to be a contributor to a book titled *The Greatest Lesson I've Ever Learned* came in the midst of this greatest difficulty in my whole life. I did not feel like writing. I started to say, "I'm sorry; I can't." But instead I heard myself saying, "I will, but I must write about what God is doing in my life right now. I have nothing else to say."

The deadline for my chapter arrived. I sent it to the publishers. I added a postscript that said, "Let me know before the book goes to print. If deliverance comes, it will be the perfect ending." I believed that was exactly what would happen. All concerned had done all they could. We were waiting on God to do His part.

The deadline for publishing the book came, and there was still no deliverance. Nevertheless I felt good that God wanted me to share my testimony of trusting Jesus in the darkness. Today I believe that's indeed what He wanted.

A WORD FROM GOD?

Time passed, and one day it became evident that the prayer we prayed was not going to be answered in the way we thought. Deliverance was not going to come in the manner we expected. I even thought I had a "word from God" right out of His Word, the Bible. It said, "Then you shall see and become radiant, and your heart shall swell with joy" (Isa. 60:5a).

I had my own interpretation of that "word." I thought it meant things were going to turn out my way. I *was sure* that my way was God's will. I could prove it to you from God's Word, and you would have agreed.

There was another factor involved, though, a problem in my neat formula. There was someone else involved. I could not choose for that person, and God will not force an individual to obey against his will. Each person must choose to do right for himself. The other person chose against the clear will of God.

Did I really get a word from God? Does God give a word that involves the choice of another individual? Does God always answer our prayers? I do believe God spoke to my heart from that passage in Isaiah. You see, after some time that Scripture *has* been fulfilled in my life. I did become radiant, and my heart swelled with great joy. But the answer did not come the way I expected or when I thought it would. I had interpreted that "word" in the light of what I thought was right and best.

Someone else had a choice that affected my interpretation. I cannot control what someone else will do. I can only pray and ask God to bring pressure to bear on that person, to bring circumstances to pass that will enable that person to make the right choices.

NOT THE ANSWER I EXPECTED

I believe God did answer my prayer. God did give many opportunities for that other person to obey. He enabled me to offer love and forgiveness and leave the way open. He has left my heart free from resentment and bitterness. I have no desire to get even. But that other person still refused to choose God's will.

God expected me and my loved ones to do our part—that's all. He would do the rest. And what a wonderful job He does and has done. I could never have figured out how God could take even those bad things and work them *together for good*.

I did, however, have to correct some of my theology concerning prayer. Our prayers do not obligate God to force someone else against his or her will to do right. They only free that person to choose.

The Lord also refined my belief about getting a "word from God." Henry Blackaby says,

> You need to be very careful about claiming you have a word from God. Claiming to have a word from God is serious busi-

ness! If you have been given a word from God, you must continue in that direction until it comes to pass (even 25 years like Abram). If you have not been given a word from God yet you say you have, you stand in judgment as a false prophet:

"You may say to yourselves, 'How can we know when a message has not been spoken by the Lord?' If what a prophet proclaims in the name of the Lord does not take place or come true, that is a message the Lord has not spoken. That prophet has spoken presumptuously" (Deut. 18:21-22). In the Old Testament law the penalty for a false prophet was death (Deut. 18:20).

That certainly is a serious charge. Do not take a word from God lightly.[1]

KNOWING GOD'S VOICE

Yes, God does want to speak to us and share His thoughts and His ways with us. Blackaby notes, "The key to knowing God's voice is not a formula. It's not a method you can follow. Knowing God's voice comes from an intimate love relationship with God."[2]

We cannot just open our Bible and choose a verse that fits our situation and say we have a word from God. If you are impressed that God is speaking to you from His Word, take that word, treasure it, and test it with time. Don't blurt out that private word God speaks to your heart for everyone to hear. Someday if it comes to pass, perhaps God will give you the liberty to share what He whispered to your heart. If not, keep it between just you and God.

"LO, THE WINTER IS PAST"

I was born and grew up in south Florida, a land of perpetual summer. I was almost forty years old before I experienced the changing of the seasons. The impact on my life the first autumn I spent in Memphis, Tennessee, was so dramatic that I have never forgotten the wonder of those thrilling days. Then came the starkness of winter. At the first freeze all of the summer flowers died, and the grass turned brown. The barrenness of winter was bleak indeed for this Florida girl.

Finally, one day I saw green leaves emerging. A jonquil peeked out; the glorious, yellow forsythia bushes exploded with color. The red buds appeared, and then the magnificent pink and white dogwood and azaleas bloomed in almost every yard and open field.

My new hometown was transformed from barrenness to beauty. It came gradually but surely. Indeed I had experienced for the first time in my life the wonder of spring. I truly am a convert to the changing of the seasons. I enjoy each of God's special times. I have even learned to appreciate the wonders of winter, but my favorite time is spring.

The circumstances of our lives can be compared to the seasons of the year. I especially think of winter and spring in this connection. Some circumstances are like the devastating cold of winter. It seems as if disappointment has turned our green leaves to brown, and then they have fallen to the ground. Sorrow has left our branches barren, and loneliness has left our ground cold and frozen.

I do not know why God allowed a bleak winter experience in my life. I gave up to Him my right to understand why this winter blew its icy wind around me, robbing me of warmth and comfort. For at least two years I woke up every morning thinking about the chill of my winter and trying to figure out why it had occurred. Finally, I gave it over to Jesus completely. I still do not understand why it happened. But I do know that I learned some lessons during this winter season.

A PURPOSE FOR EACH SEASON

God made the winter season for a purpose. The cold weather kills harmful insects that damage trees and plants. So the winter circumstances of our lives can be used by God to kill the harmful insects of selfishness, pride, misplaced priorities, lack of faith, and an attitude of lethargy.

Another reason for winter is that plants and even animals that hibernate gather strength for new growth. The old dies off, and new life comes first in bud and then full bloom. In the bleakness of winter in our hearts, we can know that God is stirring below the surface in the inner recesses in our lives. But when the winter is past, there is new life and growth. There is fresh anointing and added compassion for hurting people.

Another purpose for winter, I believe, is to provide a contrast to sameness, to make us aware of new life and beauty and blessing. In Florida I took for granted the perpetual flowers and warm weather. But now after the Tennessee winter is past, I am enthralled by the glorious spring.

BEAUTY FOR ASHES

Spring in my life brought a beautiful contrast. There was beauty for ashes, the singing of birds in my heart. There is double joy in place of double heartache. I saw the promises from God's Word that I claimed by faith burst alive in my life.

In the winter of my circumstances Jesus called to me to run into His arms for shelter and for warmth. He kept me nestled there close to Him. But now He calls to me in the spring, "Rise up, my love, my fair one, and come away. For, lo, the winter is past" (Song 2:10-11 KJV). Indeed, all things work together for good.

GET TO KNOW GOD

Oh, the mystery of prayer. We have so many questions, so many unknowns. Doesn't God already know our needs? How long should we keep on asking? Why does He answer some prayers and not others? How can we know what to pray for? Can I ask for anything I want? How many people should I enlist to pray with me? How long should I pray? Is my attitude important? Will He answer my prayers?

Even if we never know the answers to all these questions, prayer is still our spiritual lifeline. So let us examine some of the principles and promises of prayer.

First, let me encourage you to get to know this Person to whom you come with your petitions—this One we are learning to lean hard upon. He is a good God. But you must be convinced in your spirit; you must know it for yourself—not just because I say so.

PSALM 103

I memorized Psalm 103 when I was a teenager. I have read it many times during these passing years. Recently I thought through the verses of this wonderful psalm again. It is all about Him—my Lord. Of its twenty-two verses, only two are about man and his fleeting existence here on this earth. These verses are in contrast to the eternality of our great God. Verse after verse tells us what He has done and what He is like. Then we are led to bless the Lord and not to forget all His benefits to us. I'll begin this search for you:

v. 3 Who forgives all your iniquities, who heals all your diseases.

v. 4 Who redeems your life from destruction, who crowns you with lovingkindness and tender mercies.

v. 5 Who satisfies your mouth with good things.

Now I'd challenge you to complete this search on your own. Circle every reference to the Lord, including each pronoun—*who, his, he,* and *him.* Then bless the Lord over and over. Read verses 1, 2, 20-22 to Him, and thank Him that He is a good God.

This is only a beginning. The Bible is all about Him. As you learn about Him, tell Him that you love Him—that He is *your* Lord, *your* Master, *your* King.

PRAYER PROMISES

Next dig deep into God's Word and discover the prayer promises. I'll help you get started by listing a few of them.

1. The Lord Will Not Answer My Prayers If I Treasure Any Sin

> *If I regard iniquity in my heart, the Lord will not hear me.* (Ps. 66:18 KJV)

If this Scripture describes you, God has promised not to hear you, not to pay attention, when you pray. Do you have a grudge against someone, an unpaid debt, a sinful habit? Have you put someone or something before God? Have you lusted after someone else's husband or wife? Have you coveted someone else's house, car, boat, or possessions? Then God has promised not to hear your prayers. That consequence is not worth treasuring sin in your heart.

Agree with God that the sin you are harboring is wrong. Take sides with God against it. Forsake it. Ask His forgiveness; He will forgive and cleanse your heart. Only then are you on praying ground.

2. Have Faith in God

But without faith it is impossible to please Him, for he who comes to God must believe that He is, and that He is a rewarder of those who diligently seek Him. (Heb. 11:6)

The more intimately we know the Lord, the more our faith will grow. "Without faith," we are told in God's Word, "it is impossible to please Him." Jesus urged His followers to "Have faith in God" if they expected their prayers to be answered (Mark 11:22-24).

Do not have faith in yourself. A positive self-image today will turn to disappointment tomorrow. Don't be fooled by having faith in your faith. No, the Bible says, "Have faith *in God*." Keep looking to Him. He is the only one in whom we can have confidence. He cannot fail.

Are you asking, "How do I do that?" God's Word gives the answer: "So then faith comes by hearing, and hearing by the word of God" (Rom. 10:17). Yes, we are back to digging deep into God's Word. Search God's Word for illustrations and explanations of faith. They will encourage and help your faith to grow. Two of the great classics we've already noted are Hebrews 11 and Romans 10.

Some time ago I helped plan and lead a nationwide women's conference in our church with almost 4,000 in attendance. The theme was "A Flourishing Faith—in the Garden of Grace." The conference was organized around an acrostic for faith:

Fortifying faith
Accepting faith
Indwelling faith
Testifying faith
Healing faith

A biblical woman was dramatically portrayed to illustrate each type of faith.

◇ The Syrophoenician woman illustrated the need for a "fortifying faith" in the face of opposition (Mark 7:24-30).

◇ Mary, the mother of Jesus, portrayed an "accepting faith," ready to do the will of God at any cost (Luke 1:38).

◇ The woman who received an "indwelling faith" as a result of being forgiven for her many sins broke that alabaster box of ointment, anointed Jesus' feet, and washed them with her tears as an expression of great love for her Savior (Luke 7:36-50).

◇ Anna, the prophetess—a widow of about eighty-four years who served God in the Temple—showed a "testifying faith" as she spoke of Jesus to all who looked for redemption in Jerusalem (Luke 2:38).

◇ The woman with an issue of blood for twelve years pictured a "healing faith" for all who need a touch from God whether physically, emotionally, or spiritually (Luke 8:43-48).

Conference planners placed a magnificent garden with blooming plants and flowers along with a swing and a garden gate on the platform. They named it "The Garden of Grace." A modern woman coming to the "Garden of Grace" each day encountered one of the biblical women of faith. They sat down together, and the modern woman asked the biblical woman about her faith. The interviewer probed to discover how she could emulate the faith of each woman.

Then a different modern woman of faith came to each session to share her moving and relevant testimony on each type of faith. Each testimony pointed us to Jesus, "the author and finisher of our faith" (Heb. 12:2).

We praised God for His marvelous "garden of grace," which we each must enter for our own faith to grow. "For by grace are you saved through faith, and that not of yourselves; it is the gift of God, not of works, lest anyone should boast" (Eph. 2:8-9). We were challenged over and over to get into God's Word. We explored illustrations and explanations of faith. We were then encouraged to be obedient to the instructions and commands of the Lord. By these means we could come to possess a flourishing faith. So can you.

3. Ask According to God's Will

Now this is the confidence that we have in Him, that if we ask anything according to His will, He hears us. And if we know that He hears us, whatever we ask, we know that we have the petitions that we have asked of Him. (1 John 5:14-15)

No, we cannot just ask for whatever we want. We must discover what God wants and then ask Him for that. How do we make this discovery? The secret lies in the illustration Jesus gave of the vine and the branches. "If you abide in Me, and My words abide in you, you will ask what you desire, and it shall be done for you" (John 15:7).

Are we living in daily communion with Jesus? Are we living in Him, and are His words living in us? Jesus called this abiding. It is a spiritual habit we must form. It involves not only reading but meditating on and memorizing God's Word. This means consciously thinking about Him and His Word.

I'd challenge you to begin today. You cannot afford to wait. When His words become alive in you, you will be attuned to God. Only then will you be able to discern His will.

4. Ask in Jesus' Name

And in that day you will ask Me nothing. Most assuredly, I say to you, whatever you ask the Father in My name He will give you. (John 16:23)

This promise is closely related to praying in the will of God. It doesn't mean just saying, "in Jesus' name," at the end of our prayers. It means we believe Jesus would sign His name to our petitions.

Perhaps God's name is more frequently "taken in vain" in this manner than any other. We must dig deep into His Word and spend time seeking Him to know what He wants. Remember, His name is powerful and precious, but it's not a secret charm. His name represents His character.

Would your request bring honor to His name? If not, don't ask.

5. Agree with Someone Else

Again I say to you that if two of you agree on earth concerning anything that they ask, it will be done for them by My Father in heaven. For where two or three are gathered together in My name, I am there in the midst of them. (Matt. 18:19-20)

How many people should you and I enlist to pray for us for our special need? Would God be more inclined to hear us if we had a hundred or a thousand praying with us? What about those who are shut-ins and know only a few people?

The Bible does not say that the more people we have praying, the better. Neither does it say the opposite. It does, however, imply that someone else should agree. Your prayer should not just be a whim or wishful thinking.

James counsels those who are sick to call for the elders of the church to pray (James 5:14). Verse 16 says we should pray for one another. Then in Acts 12:12, we read that "many were gathered together praying" in a home for Peter's release from prison.

Perhaps the situation and circumstances determine how many should pray. Some of these questions are not clearly answered in Scripture. But of one thing I am sure: The attitude and condition of the heart are of utmost importance. James 5:16 is emphatic when it exhorts, "The effective, fervent prayer of a righteous man avails much."

KEEP ON ASKING

I do believe that if our prayers aren't answered, we should check up and see if we meet the conditions of prayer. Do we have sin in our life? Are we praying in the will of God in Jesus' name? What about our faith? Do we believe God will answer our prayers?

If we do not know of anything we should change, then Jesus gives another prayer promise: "Ask, and it will be given to you; seek, and you shall find; knock, and it will be opened to you. For everyone who asks receives, and he who seeks finds, and to him who knocks it will be opened" (Matt. 7:7-8).

Some prayers are answered immediately, some after many years. Why? Frankly, I do not claim to know the answer to this question. It is one of the great mysteries of prayer.

ASK—and keep on asking, and it shall be given to you.

SEEK—and keep on seeking, and you shall find.

KNOCK—and keep on knocking, and the door shall be opened to you.

For everyone who ASKS receives, and he who SEEKS shall find.

To him who KNOCKS, the door shall be opened.

So ASK, SEEK, KNOCK.

Learn to wait on God. We do not have to know why. God has His reasons for His delays. He is perfecting us in ways we cannot understand. Remember, He is a good God. You can trust Him. Declare along with Job, "Though He slay me, yet will I trust Him" (Job 13:15).

CLAIM ROMANS 8:28

If your prayer was not answered in the way you wanted, claim the wonderful promise of Romans 8:28 that we've already considered together. "And we know that all things work together for good to those who love God, to those who are the called according to His purpose." And know that God is good—all the time.

PRACTICING THE PROMISES

Lord, I WILL . . .

◇ Memorize and meditate on Romans 8:28.

◇ List the three worst things that have happened to me and claim Romans 8:28 in relation to them.

◇ Check up to see if I meet the conditions of answered prayer.

◇ Thank God when "my winter is past."

4

Together for Good

Leaning Hard in Times of Disappointment

~~~

Sometimes, to our great disappointment, even when we think we have met all the prayer conditions listed in the previous chapter, it becomes evident that God says no to our request. It may be that a sick loved one died even though we earnestly prayed. Or perhaps an unwanted divorce went through regardless of our prayers.

Though we do not understand, give these heartbreaks to God. Trust Him in the midst of your pain. Even the apostle Paul received a no to the prayer he prayed on three different occasions for a "thorn in the flesh" to be removed" (2 Cor. 12:7). I have wondered whether part of the reason God said no to Paul was to bolster our faith. If God denied Paul's request, then we shouldn't be so surprised when sometimes He denies ours. And just as Paul didn't lose faith, but instead declared that God's grace is sufficient, I too can keep believing, keep leaning on Jesus even when His answer is no.

In this chapter, we'll illustrate the point of believing despite all evidence to the contrary. We'll examine the real-life stories of several praying saints whose prayers were answered—but not the way they'd imagined.

A Prayer Answered Creatively

First, let me introduce you to Joseph and Elizabeth, a husband and wife who have made choices you and I can scarcely imagine, but they have seen God bring amazing answers to prayer in unforeseen ways.

Joseph Tson was a well-known Baptist pastor in Romania in the days of communist control. He broadcast the gospel all over Romania, and his writings were widely distributed.

But the Securitate began to follow him and harass him wherever he went. They beat him for his faith; however, he continued to preach the good news of Jesus. On another occasion he was called in by the Securitate and told he must comply with their wishes or suffer the consequences.

He set himself to fast and pray, and his Christian brothers and sisters joined him. He then came to his wife and said, "Elizabeth, what should I do? They have beaten me. Now they will surely kill me."

She answered, "Then Joseph, go and die, and I will die with you."

He went back to tell the man in charge of his decision.

The man replied, "You know what I can do, don't you?"

Joseph answered, "Your chief weapon is killing, but my chief weapon is dying. If you use your weapon, I will be forced to use mine. Then every sermon I've ever preached or written will be sprinkled with my blood, and everyone will be convinced that all I have preached is true."

They didn't know what to do with such a man. Later they exiled him, and he and Elizabeth came to the United States and began the Romanian Missionary Society. He had theological books translated and smuggled back into Romania to help train young pastors. He traveled extensively sharing his message on "The Doctrine of Martyrdom."

Yes, Joseph walked to the brink of death and looked over. He was willing to die for Jesus, but God preserved his life. After the Romanian revolution Joseph was among the first to return to that nation. He continues to make people aware of the need and potential of Romanian Christians to evangelize all of Europe—both east and west.

What a privilege it was more than a decade ago for my husband and me to sit in the Second Baptist Church of Oradea, Romania, and participate in the opening of the new school year at the Institute. Joseph was a man of vision and good works, and his wife, Elizabeth, was equally a woman of good works. I sat at the dinner table in Romania one evening and heard Joseph relate this story of how his wife had told him, "Joseph, go and die, and I will die with you."

I bowed my head and prayed with all my heart, "Oh, God, if You ever call upon me to face a similar situation, please let me be like Elizabeth. She is so like You."

Despite the fear, the beatings, the threats, the exile, God has worked all of these things together for good. Revival has come to Romania. Thousands are coming to Christ, and the prayers of believers were answered—not in the way or timing they probably hoped, but in ways that exceed anything they could possibly have imagined.

My Own Experience

I can attest to you that His grace is sufficient, for I have experienced this grace on many occasions. Let me share a couple of these with you. One in particular is deeply personal because I watched it happen to my very own mama.

At first I just thought that Mama was *dropping out of life.* On a return flight from visiting her, I wrote down many suggestions of things she could do to *check back into living.* I remember crying all the way home, thinking that she had somehow chosen to no longer be actively involved in life.

Then on another visit we were looking at a picture of Daddy when he was in his fifties. Mama commented, "That's Daddy when he was twenty-one years old. I used to work for him back then." Well, I knew then that something more was wrong than her choosing to drop out of living—and gradually things got worse.

The next stage was when Mama could not remember what I had told her. After some time I concluded, *Why tell Mama anything? She won't remember anyway.* But this did not satisfy me. I wanted to share my life with her.

I remember when Mama was in Memphis on one of her visits. I experienced this frustration and told Adrian, "There's just no sense in telling Mama anything anymore. She won't remember anyway."

I'll never forget his words. They pierced to my soul. "Just make her happy today. It doesn't really matter whether she remembers or not."

I had always wanted to take Mama and Daddy with us on trips—especially to the Holy Land—but they were never able to go. Now even when I told her about these trips, she never remembered what I told her. But that day I asked her, "Mama, would you like to go for a trip around the world?" She said she would. So I took her for a walk around my house and showed her my souvenirs from the Holy Land, Switzerland, and other places, telling her about each place. That evening I showed her the movies I had taken when we were in the Holy Land. She really enjoyed her "tour."

The next night I asked her if she wanted to go with me to Switzerland. Then I showed her my movies of the magnificent Swiss Alps and the waterfalls and the beautiful flowers. I will never forget those "trips" and those days, though I'm sure she did. But it did not matter anymore because I had made Mama happy *today*.

Then the time came when Mama could not come to visit anymore. But I could still visit her. I could still talk to her on the phone. She still recognized my voice. I still told her what I did. I would show her pictures of my children and my grandchildren, although I knew she would forget their names unless I reminded her.

Then one day the woman who kept her said that she could not talk on the phone anymore. And I cried; I couldn't even talk to Mama now.

The last time I went to visit Mama, she did not even call my name. But when I hugged and kissed her and smiled and told her that I loved her, her eyes lit up, and she smiled back. Then the news came: "She doesn't respond anymore. She doesn't have much time left."

And then the call—she was gone. I cried. But I had already done most of my grieving. All along the way I had found that leaning on Jesus, sharing the depth of my sorrow with Him in prayer, made the answer I received one that came from a gracious hand of a loving Father.

In His grace, He enabled me to pen a heartfelt poem that paints a picture of Mama's new reality—a picture that brought comfort to me then and even yet brings a smile.

Today Mama Knows

Today is mostly a day to rejoice!
Today Mama knows even as she is known.
She remembers everything;
She knows much more than I.
She comprehends with Christ all things;
She's completely whole!
She's gathered in the heavenly grandstands
With Daddy, little baby Philip, all her loved ones,
And with the saints of all the ages,
And most of all her Savior.

Mama, I will always remember you—
And I rejoice that now you remember all things!

RUSSELL, A BRAVE LITTLE SOLDIER

I teach a class of children who are new Christians. A few years ago I was privileged to have in my class an eight-year-old boy named Russell. He was a cancer patient. When he came to my class, he did not have any hair because of his medical treatments. One of his legs had been amputated. He originally had gone to the doctor because his parents thought he had a minor problem with his leg. It turned out not to be minor at all.

Russell and his parents lived in the town of Berryville, Arkansas, population 3,000. They had moved to Memphis for six months of treatment at the children's cancer hospital, St. Jude's.

Russell made his public profession of faith in Christ and was baptized at Bellevue. Then he attended and graduated from my children's new Christians' class. I visited him in the hospital and observed him in my class. He had great courage and faith. In fact, his faith challenged mine.

When his treatments concluded, Russell's family moved back

to Arkansas, but we continued to pray for him and to inquire about him. It wasn't long until news came that Russell had only a few days to live. I decided to call his godly young mother to tell her that we were praying for them. But guess who answered the phone? It was Russell. I was not prepared for that. I did not know exactly what to say.

I found myself asking, "How ya doin', Russell?"

He replied, "Fine, Mrs. Rogers."

I told him we were praying for him. Then I asked to speak with his mother. She took the phone into the next room and shared how the tumors were growing all over his body and were taking his life away.

In less than a week Russell went home to live with Jesus. He was a brave little soldier. The next Sunday tears filled my eyes as I told my class that Russell had died. But I reminded them that we would see Russell at that *meeting in the air* when Jesus returns. A song I loved to sing with the children was titled "There's Going to Be a Meeting in the Air." It speaks of going home to heaven and meeting both Christ and all our loved ones there. I'm glad we sang this song together because I can just envision the way it will be. On the way up I'll call out, "How ya doin', Russell?"

And I think he'll answer, "Fine, Mrs. Rogers. I'm doin' just fine!"

On that day I'm sure we'll understand how God worked it all *together for good*—even when He answered our fervent prayers with a no.

EVEN NO TURNS OUT TO BE GOOD

Like Pastor Tson, Russell, and my mama, Elisabeth Elliot went through incredibly difficult, unexplainable circumstances. In her earliest missionary days the only person qualified to help her in her Bible translation work died. After that, all her translation work was stolen. Her missionary husband, Jim Elliot, was tragically killed by the Auca Indians, and her second husband died with cancer.

When I was a young minister's wife, the Christian world was shaken by the news of the seemingly senseless killing of Jim Elliot and the others by the Auca Indians. I was deeply touched. Elizabeth's parents came to our church and spoke and showed slides during the following years.

I then read the early books Elizabeth wrote. They challenged me to be more like these missionaries who had given their lives for the gospel's sake. I could hardly believe it when I heard that Elizabeth had gone with her young daughter to live among the Aucas—those who had killed her husband.

Yes, she felt the pain of unanswered prayers. And she wrote, "Faith's most severe tests come not when we see nothing, but when we see a stunning array of evidence that seems to prove our faith vain. If God were God, if He were omnipotent, if He cared, would this have happened? One turns in disbelief again from the circumstances and looks into the abyss. But in the abyss there is only blackness, no glimmer of light, no answering echo."[1]

It was a long time before she "came to the realization that it is in our acceptance of what is given that God gives Himself."[2] By this she meant that each time we come to an end of ourselves through some type of suffering, we have an opportunity to experience more of Him. She continued, "This grief, this sorrow, this total loss that empties my hands and breaks my heart, I may, if I will, accept, and by accepting it, I find in my hands something to offer. And so I give it back to Him, who in mysterious exchange gives Himself to me."[3]

We in the evangelical world have seen God use Elisabeth Elliot in a remarkable way. To see her continue on, steadfast in her faith in God, proclaiming through the spoken word and written page her confidence in God's unchanging love, has challenged and encouraged countless lives.

In recent years I have observed how God had taken those heartbreaking circumstances and allowed Elizabeth to be a strong evangelical voice for holy living and for God's pattern for the male-female roles. I have listened to her radio broadcast that went out across the nation. She has called multitudes to be like Jesus.

When she writes about surrender, I listen. When she writes about a call to holy living, I listen. When she writes about the sufficiency of an all-knowing and all-loving God, I listen. I listen because I know she has been there.

God has given her a platform from which to speak to the world. You and I may admire her platform, but we would not want to be involved in building it. It is built of blood and sweat, tears and agony. It wasn't easy to build. It required the help of Omnipotence. Anything less would have caused a mighty fall.

Only God could have made Elisabeth Elliot Gren into *a woman like unto Himself* and used her to cause us to long to be like Him. I see in her, and in so many other modern-day heroes of the faith, the evidence of God's magnificent assurance that "all things work together for good" when we lean on Him.

PRACTICING THE PROMISES

Lord, I WILL . . .

◇ Continue to trust the Lord even when my prayers seem to go unanswered.

◇ Ask God to help me reach out to someone going through

the dark valley of divorce and show my love to that person in a practical way (call, take him or her to lunch, baby-sit, etc.).

◇ Write a note to a widow when she is lonely and encourage her to read Isaiah 54:4-14.

◇ Remember the "multitude of His mercies" when unpredictable problems come my way (Ps. 5:7; Lam. 3:32).

5

Soul-deep Restoration

From the Hand of the One on Whom We Lean

～ ～

Y ou have probably said, "Oh, my goodness!" at least as often as I have. If I asked you what you meant by that expression, you would probably reply, "Oh, nothing special."

I am not going on a crusade. But just to make you think as I have done, I want to challenge you to consider seriously what indeed *your* goodness is. As I have examined my heart, I have realized that *my* goodness is none other than God Himself. I have just been studying the names of God. But of the names listed in my study book, goodness wasn't listed. What an omission.

We need to have a solid, vivid understanding of His goodness if we are truly to come to Him in faith and lean hard on Him in times of darkness, difficulty, and questioning. If He's not good, then what's the use of trying to lean on Him? If He's not good, then maybe He's capricious, or maybe He rejoices in our pain. What good would it be to try to lean on someone like that?

But He's not like that. He is good. All the time. Just to be sure we know this deep down, let's remind ourselves of what His Word says about His goodness.

In your name I will hope, for your name is good (Ps. 52:9 NIV).

Good and goodness are both descriptions and names for God.

The earth is full of the goodness of the LORD. (Ps. 33:5)

Oh, how great is Your goodness, which You have laid up for those who fear You. (Ps. 31:19)

I would have lost heart, unless I had believed that I would see the goodness of the LORD in the land of the living. (Ps. 27:13)

My people shall be satisfied with My goodness. (Jer. 31:14)

They shall utter the memory of Your great goodness. (Ps. 145:7)

Or do you despise the riches of His goodness, forbearance, and longsuffering, not knowing that the goodness of God leads you to repentance? (Rom. 2:4)

HIS NAMES ARE ALL GOOD

Besides Good and Goodness being specific names for God, all of His names are good. They are the expressions of His unequalled goodness—He defines goodness; without Him no goodness could exist. God's names tell who He is and what He does. Everything we need is described in one of His wonderful names.

Blessings come as we consider His names, as we ponder and meditate on their meanings. But He will come alive in us as we claim, as we appropriate, all that they mean in our particular circumstances. He is waiting to be our Comforter, our Peace, our Savior, our Refuge, our Judge, our Good Shepherd, our Holy One, our heavenly Bridegroom, and much, much more.

In another Bible study in which I was enrolled, we were all challenged to write our own version of the Twenty-third Psalm, using for the theme what Jesus meant most to us at that time. (The study was of the book *Experiencing God* by Henry T. Blackaby and Claude V. King.)

Because my chief role is that of wife and homemaker, I chose Bridegroom and Husband for my theme. What a blessing it was to consider what Jesus means to me by these names. Let me share with you what I wrote in the hopes that this will challenge you to consider in a specific way what He means to you as you meditate on His good names.

My Twenty-third Psalm

The Lord is my Bridegroom and my Husband;
I shall not lack love and companionship.

He gives me understanding of His ways;
He understands all my needs and desires.
He longs to spend time to fellowship with me;
He leads me into quiet times with Him alone.

Yes, though I'm surrounded by rejection and loneliness,
I will fear no evil; for You are with me.
I know that You love me, for I feel Your presence,
and I hear Your voice.

You loved me so much that You laid down Your life for me;
You provide for every need I have;
You protect me from those who would do me harm.
Surely Your goodness and lovingkindness
will be evident every day I live,

*And I shall be united with my heavenly Bridegroom
and Husband forever.*

A Prescription to Restore Your Soul

My friend Charles is a doctor; so when it came time to teach his son a lesson about depending on Jesus, he took out a prescription pad and prescribed this dose: "Read the Twenty-third Psalm three times a day (out loud) for at least a week." Charles had come across this idea in a book, and this application of it became the beginning of his son's return to a closer walk with the Lord.

As I pondered this situation, I wondered why the young man had responded to this suggestion when he had neglected so many others. Allowing for circumstances that only God may know, it seemed to me that one secret to his completing this assignment was that it was simple—yet profound.

The more I thought about this idea, the more I determined to do it myself. So I read the psalm—three times a day (out loud) for a week. I had memorized this wonderful psalm as a child, and I am so familiar with it that sometimes its profundity slips by. The reason, I'm sure, for reading or quoting the psalm out loud is to overcome this danger.

The first day I thought, *I'll circle with my pen every reference to the Lord, even every pronoun.* The following day I underlined every verb that told what the Lord would do. Then the next day I marked every personal pronoun. The Lord began to make this psalm personal to me.

I then began to pray the psalm for myself, claiming its promises: "Lord, You are my Shepherd (my Good Shepherd); You have promised that I shall not want. Make me lie down in Your green pastures. Lord, lead me beside Your still waters. Give me the guidance I so badly need today. Restore my soul—renew me; correct me. Lead me in Your path of righteousness, not for my sake—but for the love of Your name." And so on.

After a few days, this familiar psalm became new and alive and exciting. I began to study about the relationship of sheep and their shepherd to see what more I could learn. I added other resources, showing what others had gained from this life-changing passage of Scripture. The more I read, the more I wanted to continue.

When the week ended, I did not see how I could quit. The Lord laid it on my heart to pray it in behalf of my daughter Gayle. Three times a day (out loud) for a week I prayed and claimed this psalm in her behalf. "Lord, make her to lie down in green pastures; lead her beside still waters; lead her in the paths of righteousness for Your name's sake."

A couple of weeks later I felt impressed to tell her of my prayer for her. I discovered that she and her family were considering a major move. Even before she told us about it, the Lord had led me to pray for His leadership in her life. What a blessing to lean on this Shepherd who knows what we and our loved ones need even when we don't have a clue.

The next week I prayed it for my son Steve and then for my son David. Then I prayed it in behalf of my daughter Janice. I discovered that she was considering a move back home. She had said, "Don't get too excited because we don't know for sure, but we may be moving back home to Memphis. Will you pray?" Indeed I would; in fact, I had already been praying for leadership in her life by her Good Shepherd—Jesus Christ.

Next I prayed it for my husband. Since then I have prayed it through on numerous occasions for friends and loved ones who were going through difficult times. My neighbor's husband died, and I told her about the psalm and prayed it for her. Two precious couples lost their babies. I claimed its promises for them. A friend had cancer surgery; so it became my prayer for her. A close friend buried her husband, and I prayed, "Lord, though Kathy is walking through the valley of the shadow of death, may she fear no evil. May Your rod and staff comfort her. Anoint her with the oil of Your Holy Spirit, and may her cup run over with joy."

I do not know when I will stop praying the Twenty-third Psalm every day. I prayed it three times a day for two months. At this writing four months have passed. I have continued to pray it at least once a day for myself or for someone else going though some hardship.

I cannot begin to tell you what blessing this practice has brought to my life. I have shared this idea with many others, as it had been shared with me. Let me challenge you to do the same.

Here is your prescription for the restoration of your soul. Read or quote and pray the Twenty-third Psalm (out loud) three times a day for at least the next week. I will guarantee you, if your heart attitude is attuned to your Lord, it will transform your life.

I said earlier that this psalm held blessing and insight for me in a way I'd never have believed. Allow me to share some insights I have gained in these months of renewal through the Twenty-third Psalm.

THE GOOD SHEPHERD

The LORD is my shepherd: I shall not want. (Ps. 23:1)

Sheep hold a fascination for me. The first time I ever saw a flock of sheep on a hillside was when I traveled in the Holy Land as a grown woman. I watched them with intensity. You see, sheep are not just another breed of animal, but they are closer to me somehow because they are right out of the pages of my favorite book, the Bible. I had read about them since I was a child but had never seen them on a hillside.

This flock represented spiritual lessons and truths. God's Word had told me that I am like a sheep. "All we like sheep have gone astray; We have turned, every one, to his own way"(Isa. 53:6). A picture I remember from childhood was of Jesus reaching down over a cliff to rescue a lost sheep. That lost sheep represented me. Another picture I recall was of Jesus carrying a wounded lamb on His shoulders, taking it back to the fold. That was also me.

I always loved the story in Matthew 18:11-14 that pictures Jesus as the Good Shepherd. He left the ninety-nine in the safety of the fold and went out to look for the one lost sheep—another picture of my condition before He rescued me.

Yes, I had loved those pictures since I was a child. Now before my eyes was a "living picture." I strained to catch a glimpse of the shepherd who was leading his sheep. Finally someone called out, "There's the shepherd." Yes, there he was, right there beside the sheep, doing all the things I'd read about in Psalm 23. Leading. Guiding. Feeding. Bringing water and rest and protection to his flock.

A good shepherd manifests his character by staying with the sheep. "The good shepherd gives His life for the sheep" (John 10:11). The hireling flees when he sees the wolf coming. He doesn't care for the sheep.

The ultimate proof of Jesus' goodness is when He laid down His life for us, His sheep. Yes, God the Father laid on Jesus the iniquity of us all (Isa. 53:6b). In exchange He made us like Him and gave us His goodness.

The Person of this goodness is the Shepherd of the Twenty-third Psalm. "The LORD is my shepherd" (Ps. 23:1). The Good

Shepherd is revealed in John 10 as none other than Jesus Himself. We will also look closely at His character and His crucifixion, for they are inextricably interwoven.

Through the years since then, I have seen sheep in many different situations. I have seen them grazing on the hillside, drinking water from a trough, coming through a narrow valley, and sheltered safely in the fold. I am still intrigued by these woolly animals that Jesus used to represent you and me.

Now when I see a flock of sheep, I always look for the shepherd. I know he is near, for sheep can't get along without him. And every time I see a shepherd, I think of my Shepherd. How precious to me is the Shepherd of my soul.

FRESH GREEN PASTURES

He makes me to lie down in green pastures. (Ps. 23:2)

The shepherd must diligently search for good provisions for his sheep. He must rise early, often by 3 A.M., because sheep graze better in the early hours of the day while the dew is still on the grass. They cannot graze in the same pasture day after day. They must keep on the go, always looking for fresh green pastures. To find these precious provisions, the shepherd may have to climb rocky mountains, traverse narrow passes, and plod through giant fields of thorns and thistles.

The sheep also must have fresh, clean water to drink. The shepherd must lead them beside still waters. He must find a place of shade for them to rest from the scorching sun.

Just like this shepherd in the Holy Land, our Good Shepherd Jesus has made good provision for us. He gives us all the spiritual resources we need to keep us growing. And to illustrate that and remind us of His provision in this most important spiritual realm,

He created a good physical world for us. Everything about it was good until sin entered the Garden of Eden. Even now it retains many good provisions.

He gave to His chosen people a good land—the land of Canaan. This land was especially amazing to those in that first generation who came from bondage in Egypt to the Promised Land. It was a land filled with many good things to eat and drink. These good things represent spiritual provisions to keep us growing.

God makes provisions for His children in many different ways. Some are magnificent—the awesome beauty of a sunset or the snow-capped mountain peaks. Others are mundane—daily bread to eat and water to drink.

Some provisions are given to everyone. "He makes His sun rise on the evil and on the good, and sends rain on the just and on the unjust" (Matt. 5:45). Others are uniquely designed with just you and me in mind. Whichever kind they are, they are expressions of God's goodness. He gives to us good gifts—good things. "Blessed be the Lord, who daily loads us with benefits, the God of our salvation" (Ps. 68:19).

"FOR HIS NAME'S SAKE"

He restores my soul; He leads me in the paths of righteousness for His name's sake. (Ps. 23:3)

The shepherd lives with the welfare and enrichment of his flock ever in mind. Many times he picks a sheep up and lays it over his shoulders to carry it. The lambs he carries in his bosom. He puts them on the right path. Then he corrects, restores, and leads them safely home.

When the shepherd rescues the wayward, battered sheep, he does not drive it, but he leads it. If the sheep cannot make it up a steep cliff, the shepherd reaches down his crook and lifts it up. He is always lifting his sheep. But they must choose to follow the good shepherd, and we must choose to follow our Good Shepherd.

Bill and Gloria Gaither wrote a song titled "Gentle Shepherd" several years back. The lyrics remind us of our dependence upon God. But the image of Christ as our "Gentle Shepherd" is something that resonates in my soul. He gently restores, gently leads, gently brings healing to my suffering heart.

Why does the shepherd go to all this bother? He does not do it because the sheep deserve it. In fact, they are an awful lot of trouble and are always getting themselves into some kind of mess. They may wander onto a high cliff or fall into a horrible pit. They may fall over and be cast down so that they cannot even get up by themselves.

The Bible tells us that our Good Shepherd, Jesus Christ, rescues and restores us. Why? He does it for His name's sake. His character is expressed in His name. He wants us to choose to be like Him.

His name is so important that God keeps a special Book of Remembrance for those who reverence Him and think upon His name. It is being written in the presence of God. "A book of remembrance was written before Him for those who fear the LORD and who meditate on His name" (Mal. 3:16b).

As we come to know His name—yes, His many names—we learn about His character. As we meditate on who He is, we come to know and love Him intimately. As we gaze upon Him, we become like Him. "But we all, with unveiled face, beholding as in a mirror the glory of the Lord, are being transformed into the same image from glory to glory, just as by the Spirit of the Lord" (2 Cor. 3:18).

Oh, how I love His name. I love to sing praises to His name.

I love to speak His name in love and prayer. He does not drive but leads us. But we must choose to follow Him.

"Thou Art with Me"

Yea, though I walk through the valley of the shadow of death, I will fear no evil: for thou art with me; thy rod and thy staff they comfort me. (Ps. 23:4 KJV)

One of the awesome experiences in the Holy Land is to ride through the area known as the Valley of the Shadow of Death in the wilderness of the Judean desert. This valley is nothing but miles of stark, barren hills and ravines.

One deep, narrow valley is especially treacherous. As I looked through the zoom lens of my video camera, I could just catch a glimpse of a flock of sheep coming through the dangerous pass, led by their shepherd. It was exciting to watch this scene so like the one the psalmist describes. I thought of our Good Shepherd, the master communicator of spiritual truth, who said, "And when he brings out his own sheep, he goes before them; and the sheep follow him, for they know his voice" (John 10:4).

Not only does the shepherd show the way through the valley, but he provides protection for the sheep. If a wolf comes to steal or kill the sheep, the shepherd is willing to put his own life between the thief and the sheep—willing to die for them. At night the shepherd lies down in the opening of the fold. He becomes the door of the sheepfold. Any enemy would have to climb over his body.

Our Good Shepherd willingly laid down His life for us, His sheep. If we are in Christ, Satan would have to climb over Him to get to us. Praise God, we can be sure we are eternally secure in His protection.

I have known His presence in this dark, treacherous valley.

Therefore, I am able to give this assurance to those of you who are right now walking through a lonesome narrow place.

"IN THE PRESENCE OF MY ENEMIES"

You prepare a table before me in the presence of my enemies;
You anoint my head with oil; My cup runs over. (Ps. 23:5)

A shepherd will often find a tableland of green, flourishing grass, a place where a mountain shades the grass from the hot sun. He then prepares it before he lets his sheep graze there.

He looks for poisonous weeds and carries them away. He runs off ravenous beasts. He looks for viper holes. If a sheep were struck by a viper, it would die in two minutes. The shepherd pours oil around the hole and lets it run down into it because a viper cannot make it up the slippery hole.

As the shepherd prepares the tableland of grass in the presence of the sheep's enemies, so our Good Shepherd prepares a table for us right when our enemy is near. God runs the so-called good and bad alongside each other if only we have eyes to see. Do not fail to enjoy the banquet God prepares even when the enemy is lurking in the shadows.

After the shepherd brings his sheep back to the fold at night, he examines each one carefully for wounds. If he finds any, he anoints them with oil for healing and to stop infection. This anointing also protects them from the extreme heat of the day.

On one occasion in the Holy Land, our guide pointed out a watering trough. He told us this was what was referred to as the cup of the Twenty-third Psalm. The shepherd would draw water from the well and pour it into the watering trough. Then the sheep would stick its nose into that water right up to its eyes and drink. The fresh, cool water would overflow the rim of the cup.

When I was going through one of the most difficult times in my life, one of the greatest moments of victory and blessing was facing me also. We were moving into a brand-new church building with special celebration services. I had to choose to enjoy the blessing. I made that choice by faith, and my heart experienced overwhelming peace and joy despite my inner turmoil. Yes, my cup overflowed with blessing, just as He said.

Some time ago I attended a wedding where the bride had chickenpox. The doctor said she could go ahead with the wedding. I observed the bride, the groom, and the entire family deal with this less-than-desirable circumstance. They were able to be joyful and radiant in the presence of this enemy. They had chosen by faith to rejoice.

As I sat in the auditorium before the bride entered, I looked around and saw the beautiful flowers. I listened to the magnificent music and thought, *What a wonderful banquet table has been prepared even when the enemy is near.* With the "miracle" of makeup, you could not even see the bride's chickenpox. She was beautiful, and the groom was smiling when he said, "in sickness and in health." Yes, He gives peace in every circumstance.

"SURELY GOODNESS AND MERCY"

Surely goodness and mercy shall follow me all the days of my life; and I will dwell in the house of the LORD forever. (Ps. 23:6)

David begins the final reminder of this psalm with the word *surely*. This assurance is based on God's unfailing promise that He will be our Shepherd. His goodness and mercy will follow us from the days of our youth to the very end. David also said in Psalm: 71:5-6: "For You are my hope, O Lord GOD; *You are* my trust from my youth. By You I have been upheld from birth; You are He who took me out of my mother's womb."

David no doubt remembered many times when, as a young shepherd lying under the star-lit Judean skies, he had meditated upon the Lord, his Good Shepherd. David had not always been faithful, but God had been faithful to him. David recognized God's goodness. How thankful he was for the multitude of God's mercies. "Hear me, O LORD, for Your lovingkindness *is* good; turn to me according to the multitude of Your tender mercies" (Ps. 69:16).

I can echo these words of the psalmist. Yes, goodness and mercy have followed me all the days of my life. Praise God for His unfailing promise. I'm counting on it.

Yes, my baby Philip is there with Jesus, Mama and Daddy, and other loved ones. Jesus is there to welcome us all home. Yes, heaven is nearer and dearer now—with loved ones gone on ahead.

Right before my precious friend Virginia died, heaven was so real to me that I leaned down low and whispered to her, "When you get to heaven, would you please say hello to Philip for me." She said she would.

What a prospect—to spend eternity in paradise with my Good Shepherd who has led me all the way home. Jesus offered a place in Paradise to the trusting thief on the cross. He now offers us a glorious place that He's prepared for you and me.

His goodness goes on forever, but the question remains, "What does He mean to me?" Can I say in all sincerity, "Oh, *He* is my goodness"? For within me is no good thing. He is my only hope for goodness.

Praise God, His name is Good. His name is Goodness, and He is our Good Shepherd. The next time someone (maybe it will be you) says, "Oh, my goodness," let it be a reminder to silently pray, *Thank You, Lord, that You are my Goodness.*

PRACTICING THE PROMISES

Lord, I WILL . . .

◇ Read Psalm 23 aloud every day for at least a week, remembering to make it my own and to use it as a prayer for myself and my loved ones.

◇ Memorize Malachi 3:16 and desire for my name to be written in God's Book of Remembrance.

◇ Stop to ponder on who my Goodness is the next time I say, "Oh, my goodness."

◇ Make a list of twelve of God's names, and meditate on one of them each month.

◇ Read John 10 and meditate on Jesus, my Good Shepherd.

◇ List five of God's good provisions to me that are "magnificent in scope."

◇ List five of God's good provisions to me that are "mundane in nature."

◇ Remind myself when something bad happens that God is good all the time.

6

God's Desire for Me

*Leaning on Jesus
When the Gifts Are Good*

⁓ ⁓

It was the Christmas season in 1985. I awoke one morning thinking about what I needed to *do* to finish my preparation for Christmas rather than thinking about my Lord. I then consciously decided that the busyness of Christmas would not push out the preeminence of Christ.

I had already decided I would spend the Christmas season reviewing the Gospels, focusing on Jesus, my Lord and Savior. I turned in my Bible to Matthew 7 and began to read. It was verse 11 that arrested my attention: "If you then, being evil, know how to give good gifts to your children, how much more will your Father who is in heaven give good things to those who ask Him!"

That reminded me that I was in the midst of my Christmas shopping. The main reason I wasn't finished was that I was concerned that each gift for my children and grandchildren, loved ones and friends be a good gift—something each one needed and wanted.

I had carefully shopped for small items I could send airmail to my son David, serving on a missionary ship overseas. I wanted the gifts to convey the message, "I love you and miss you this Christmas." So several weeks before, I had mailed a package to Italy that contained guitar strings, a small alarm clock, Christmas decorations, and a bag of homemade Christmas cookies and goodies. Yes, we know how to give good gifts to our children.

But the verse says, "how much more" shall your Father in heaven give good things to those who ask Him. *How much more!* Good things. If I think I care about giving good gifts, then I should understand something of God's desire for me.

I cannot begin to comprehend His "how much more." But God gave me a wonderful example in the gifts I'd sent to David. My son had been overseas for a year and a half. He had made a two-year commitment to serve on a ship that traveled to various ports in Europe sharing the gospel.

For the last five months they had been in Spain. While David was there, an opportunity arose for him to stay in Spain for a year instead of remaining with the ship as it proceeded around the coast of Africa. We were all praying with David.

I became excited about this prospect when I discovered that if he remained in Spain, we would be allowed to fly him home from Thanksgiving through Christmas. I felt God had planned it all, for all the rest of our family was coming for Christmas. Now *everyone* would be home for Christmas for the first time in years.

This would be possible because the year in Spain wouldn't begin until January, and a year on the ship would end in October. Days turned into months as we waited and prayed. I put all planning on hold until we heard David's decision. As we wrote and prayed and talked by phone, it became obvious to us all that God was leading David to stay with the ship to participate in Project Africa. We were glad—but sad at the same time.

I was happy he was going to Africa, but I fought back tears when I talked to him on the phone. When I hung up, I sat in my husband's lap and cried as I said, "It's all right. I just have to cry."

ALMOST TOO GOOD TO BE TRUE

One day my husband asked me what I wanted for Christmas. I replied, "A trip to see David." If that was not possible, I would be content. (It was only by faith at first.) My husband's schedule was so busy that even if everything else worked out, it would be most difficult to find a time to leave.

Then on Thanksgiving Day we called David to check his schedule. With some planning and adjusting, we came up with a time. And then a miracle. Through the graciousness of a friend two free trips to Italy were given to us. I could hardly believe it. And to top it all, we would arrive on my birthday, January 28. It was almost too good to be true.

As I was reading Matthew 7:11, God reminded me of His "how much more." Yes, "how much more," indeed, had the Father in heaven given a good gift to us!

I don't always understand the ways God works, but I know that I know that I know that He is a good God who gives good things. I must trust Him when those things are seen or unseen—when things turn out to agree with my comprehension of good and when they do not. Yes, all things work together for good.

Fast-forward eight years to October 1993. By this time David and his young family had spent three Christmases in Spain as missionary church planters. Another Christmas season was approaching. I had looked at our calendar to see if we could be with them their fourth Christmas away from home, but it seemed impossible. My heart ached when I thought about it, but I knew

I would have to give this longing to God—and lean on Him despite my disappointment.

After all, we were able to visit them on several occasions in Spain. What joyous times they had been. Then one day David said over the phone, "Mother, don't get too excited yet, but we may be coming home soon, taking an early furlough." Well, what does a mother do with that kind of remark?

When I hung up the phone, I jumped up and down and said to my husband, "Why not get excited today? If they can't come, I can handle that tomorrow."

On our next phone call I cautiously asked, "Son, do you think you'll be home for Christmas?"

And he replied, "Yes." Well, do you think I got excited? You'd better believe it! My son was coming home for Christmas. Kelly and little Jonathan would be here, too.

I couldn't help remembering that Christmas eight years ago when I had to give to God my expectation for David's coming home for Christmas. And now this unexpected gift of God's goodness. Home for Christmas. *Oh, God, You are, oh, so good.* All things indeed work together for good when you're leaning on Jesus.

PRACTICING THE PROMISES

Lord, I WILL . . .

◇ List five concrete examples of God's great goodness to me.

◇ Make a list of twelve of God's names, one for each month, and meditate on one of them each month. Write them on a calendar.

◇ Sing "God Is So Good" every day for a week. (I will personalize it and also sing, "God, You're So Good.")

◇ Read the story of the creation in Genesis 1. Circle this phrase each time it appears: "God saw that it was good" and the one phrase, "Behold, it was very good." Just think about that!

◇ Sing to the Lord "I Sing the Mighty Power of God" or "How Great Thou Art," meditating on the magnificence of His creation.

◇ Read Psalm 104 aloud. Then circle the pronouns *Who*, *Thou*, and *He* and underline what He has done in relation to creation. Finally, then, praise the Lord for each thing He has done by reading out loud each pronoun circled and each phrase underlined.

7

Choosing to Become Like Jesus

Leaning on Jesus for Direction

~ ~

The uniqueness of God's magnificent creation, mankind, is the ability to choose. This ability holds the potential for good or evil. It is God's tool for testing. Adam and Eve were the original pair who made the first choice. They failed the test. They chose to take the forbidden fruit and suffered the consequences.

The ability to choose is a priceless gift of God. We should not take it for granted, but treasure and protect it. We take notice of this gift when our precious toddler begins to reach for our breakable coffee table treasures, and we say, "No!" The contest then begins. Whatever is forbidden becomes the thing desired.

I have a precious grandson, Michael, who is now eighteen years old. I still remember when he was at the peak of his first testing period (eighteen months old). He failed frequently. He liked to reach for my little ivory elephants and handmade pinecone duck. He also had a two-month-old brother, Adrian, whom he liked to poke.

This early choosing time is critical to the training of a child. If he makes the wrong choices, he must suffer the consequences. When Michael passed the test and made a good choice, his parents encouraged him and even rewarded him at times. Good choices are a sign of maturity, and we all rejoice at each good choice.

Michael has now passed through more choices and stages and has learned that each stage of life holds its major choices. If we pass the tests of each period, the choices associated with that stage are no longer major. There are then the choices unique to the next stage. If we make good choices, we keep progressing to maturity.

Choices are associated with every area of our lives—the physical, emotional, and spiritual. We can be mature in one area and stunted in another. Good physical choices will not produce spiritual maturity. These areas do interrelate with one another, but we still must make clear-cut choices in each area.

Why all this talk about choices in a book about leaning on Jesus? Shouldn't we focus our attention only on Him and nothing else. Well, yes. But that, too, is a choice. Depending on Him is a choice. Leaning takes an act of our wills. And choosing to become like Him in our leaning brings pleasure to our Creator. It is truly our gift back to Him.

Reputation or Riches

One of the most critical of all choices concerns our reputation. In fact, a reputation is the end result of all the choices we make. When we were young, our parents trained us to make good choices. In this early testing period we could choose to obey or disobey. "Even a child is known by his deeds, whether what he does is pure and right" (Prov. 20:11).

One of the major opportunities to make choices comes as we grow up and discover what riches can purchase for us on this earth. Riches are meaningless to a young child, although he might be the recipient of comfort and convenience. He could be just as happy on a straw mat as a Beautyrest mattress. We didn't have a lovely decorated nursery for our two older children, as we did for our two younger. But the older ones didn't know or care. In fact, unless we are destitute, with our basic needs unmet, it is only as we grow older and see what others have in comparison to what we have that we are tempted to choose to be discontented.

I remember when I was ten years old, I thought I had had a marvelous Christmas—until I went to my best friend's house and saw that she had received almost twice as much as I. It was my choice to be contented or discontented.

As I look back on my teenage years, I realize what beautiful clothes my mother sewed for me. She even made my lovely wedding dress. But at the time I thought I was not as fortunate as some of my friends who had store-bought clothes. I can remember that I couldn't wait until I had saved enough of my allowance to purchase a store-bought dress. Another choice.

As long as I can remember, I have treasured having a good reputation—far before I faced the choice between enjoying my friend's bounty with her or being jealous of her good fortune. I'm sure that this value of reputation was rooted in my family heritage.

I was never ashamed of my family name. My daddy had built a good reputation, and he handed it down to me. I was happy to carry on this family tradition. My daddy is no longer alive. Someone else now owns the business he built for thirty-five years. But my daddy's reputation was so good that the man who bought the business continued to use Daddy's name—Gentry Bros. Paint and Glass Co. However, just because Daddy chose to build a good name was not sufficient for my reputation. He was certainly a good example, but I had to make the choice myself.

When our children were younger, as they left for school or a date, we often said, "Remember who and whose you are." This had a double meaning, and they soon understood. They were to remember the good family name they bore. They all received Christ at an early age; so it also meant, "Don't forget that you bear the name Christian, and you represent Christ's family name and reputation. Never do anything to embarrass Jesus or us." It's a great family tradition. My children are also carrying it on. Our grandchildren and their children will continue it on and on, I trust. One grandchild, Adrian Foster, was named after my husband. His Papa will frequently remind him to "take care of his name."

How sad when we hear of someone who sullies his family name. It always seems to make the newspaper if a child of the rich and famous gets arrested for drugs or DUI. We recognize the family name.

But how much more tragic it is when a child of God falls into immoral or dishonest behavior and sullies Christ's family name. The news media delights to broadcast far and wide that incident that brings reproach on Christ's name. In recent times when some well-known Christian leaders brought shame on Christ's name, all of us in His family suffered shame and sorrow. How my heart ached as I heard talk show hosts ridicule the cause of Christ because of a few who did not choose a good name over riches, fame, or pleasure.

Yes, some are known for their bad choices. But there are many who are known by their good choices. How grateful I am for their examples. The Bible says, "The steps of a good man are ordered by the LORD, and He delights in his way" (Ps. 37:23).

I can't remember the day or time when I began to choose a

good name over riches. I just know I have made that choice and continue to make it daily. It's a good choice—the right choice, the God-honoring choice. And it's one modeled by men and women of God—from Bible times and even from today's world. Let me introduce you to a few of them.

DORCAS—FULL OF GOOD WORKS

The story of Dorcas is found in the ninth chapter of Acts. She is described as a woman "full of good works and charitable deeds which she did" (Acts 9:36).

The story continues that when she died, "all the widows stood by him [Peter] weeping, showing the tunics and garments which Dorcas had made while she was with them" (Acts 9:39b).

A mighty miracle was worked that day as she was raised from the dead, and that is what we tend to hear about in church and Bible study classes, as well we should. But it should also be noted that Dorcas had spent a lifetime building a good name. She was known for her good works—the people she had helped.

Today in our church, as in many churches, we have a ladies' Sunday school class named after her, called the Dorcas Class or the Dorcas Circle. She is still an example to us, demonstrating devotion and leaning on Jesus in tangible, outward acts that bring credit to Him.

MISS NOBIE—A MODERN-DAY DORCAS

Nobie Moore, a widow of many years, lovingly known as "Miss Nobie," was a member of our church for fifty-nine years. Although widowed at an early age, she never seemed to feel sorry for herself. She had to work to support herself, but she was always faithful to her church. She invited young girls to her house on

Saturdays for pancakes. They brought the pancake mix, syrup, and strawberries. She trained them in Scripture memory and Christian living.

At one time she sewed a homemade apron for each woman who became a new member of our church. She also sewed hundreds of aprons and sent them to missionaries and their daughters. I have one of those treasured aprons in my kitchen.

Before she graduated to glory, she wrote an average of eight to ten letters a day to missionaries, and she prayed for them and others daily. I feel blessed to have been included on her daily prayer list. Her name will never be on the national news, but it is written in God's Hall of Fame. I want to be more like "Miss Nobie"—a good woman who chose to be full of good works as she leaned hard on Jesus.

CORNELIUS—A GOOD REPUTATION

The story of Cornelius is found in chapter 10 of Acts: "Cornelius the centurion, a just man, one who fears God and has a good reputation among all the nation of the Jews" (v. 22). He was a Gentile, a military man, but he did not have a dictatorial, harsh manner. He was described as "a devout man and one who feared God with all his household, who gave alms generously to the people, and prayed to God always" (vv. 1-2).

He wasn't a Christian, but he had a heart for God and sought to the best of his ability to know Him. God honored his desire, and sent Peter to his house with the good news of Jesus Christ. Everyone there that day, including Cornelius, was saved and baptized and filled with the Holy Spirit.

We usually remember this story because of Peter's vision of unclean animals and God's lesson that no person is common or unclean. Sometimes we overlook the good reputation of this man—a man with a heart for God.

GOOD WORKS—THE RESULT, NOT THE CAUSE

For He made Him who knew no sin to be sin for us, that we might become the righteousness of God in Him. (2 Cor. 5:21)

The great continental divide in Christian denominations is created by three important prepositions and three important nouns: By—grace. Through—faith. Unto—good works.

You and I are just sinners saved by grace. But by that I don't mean that therefore I will excuse myself to go on sinning. No, it's not, "Poor me; I'm so weak that I can't help but sin." No, what I mean is that without Jesus I am nothing: I'm a sinner. I've fallen short of God's glory.

Two great truths I have learned in my Christian life are these: "Without [Jesus I] can do nothing" (John 15:5b); and "I can do all things through Christ who strengthens me" (Phil. 4:13). It is He who strengthens and equips us to do the good deeds of Dorcas or Miss Nobie or Cornelius.

Yes, I was a sinner, but I now possess an exchanged life. Perhaps this example will help you understand a bit about the exchange. I'm a part of a staff wives' fellowship that has a custom of exchanging Christmas ornaments each year. We enjoy looking at each ornament as it is unwrapped. But we all agreed to purchase gifts of similar value to make it an equal exchange.

Jesus' exchange is far different. It is an *un*equal exchange. Jesus took my sins; and in exchange, He gave me His goodness. Remember, I had no goodness of my own. And He had no sin. But He made the exchange so that I might become the righteousness of God in Him. This exchange was not because of me, but because of Him. I had to give up my sins, but in exchange He gave me His goodness.

Yes, I believe in doing good works. I believe in the Ten Commandments and the Sermon on the Mount and the Golden Rule. But I believe that good works are the *result* of my salvation and not the cause. Titus 3:5b says salvation is "not by works of righteousness which we have done, but according to His mercy He saved us." Paul tells Titus "that those who have believed in God should be careful to maintain good works. These things are good and profitable to men" (Titus 3:8b).

We are told in Philippians 2:12 to "work out your own salvation." Paul did not say, "work for your salvation." He said, "It is God who works in you both to will and to do for His good pleasure" (v. 13). God works it in, and we work it out in our lives. Oswald Chambers put it this way: "working out what God has worked in."[1]

The secret of a life of good works is illustrated in the vine and the branch (John 15:1-8). Jesus is the true Vine. He is the source of our life. But if we are to bear fruit (good works), we must abide in the vine. We must receive our life from Him, and His life will flow through us. Then we will bear the fruit of the Spirit.

Others will come along and see this beautiful fruit. We can then say, "Help yourself to some love—the love of Jesus, the joy of the Lord, the peace of God. Then they will come to know Him as they too feed on this delicious fruit that He produces in our lives.

Abiding in Jesus is the secret to fruit-bearing. It is the secret also to answered prayer: "If you abide in Me, and My words abide in you, you will ask what you desire, and it shall be done for you" (John 15:7). We abide by faith—believing God. Think of how compatible the concepts of leaning and abiding truly are. Both concepts call us to live inside the circle of His love and His will.

Both require a closeness to Him—a beautiful, joyful closeness. And both concepts require faith, dependence, and trust.

Our faith grows as we feed on the meat of His Word. No, we are not saved by works, but by a faith that works. Works are the proof, not the prerequisite of our salvation. Yes, it is true that "faith without works is dead" (James 2:20).

GOOD WORKS FOR WHOM?

So, then, who should be the beneficiaries of the good works in our lives that will grow as we lean and abide?

Orphans and widows (James 1:27). God calls His people to demonstrate His love tangibly to those who have lost their earthly provider. Will we demonstrate to these that Jesus is their *Jehovah Jireh* (our *provider*)?

Aged parents (Mark 7:9-13). God's Word also says, "But if anyone does not provide for his own, and especially for those of his household, he has denied the faith and is worse than an unbeliever" (1 Tim. 5:8). We are expected to provide for those who provided for us. In Bible times the Pharisees and scribes followed the letter of the law, but Jesus said their hearts were far from Him. They rejected God's commandments and followed their own tradition. Instead of honoring their fathers and mothers as God had commanded, they found a man-made loophole to excuse themselves from the responsibility of caring for their aged parents. They said, "It is Corban." (In other words, "I have dedicated to God that which would relieve their need" [as described in Mark 7:11].) The religious leaders then excused themselves them from using their money and provisions for their parents. But no self-justification of this self-righteous attitude could excuse them from obeying God's command—at least not in Jesus' eyes.

The sick (Acts 4:9-10). Peter and John healed the sick in the name of Jesus. We should follow their example and care for those who are sick around us, bringing healing to their bodies and souls.

Husbands, children, in everyday living (Prov. 31:12). It is said about the virtuous wife of Proverbs 31 that "she does him [her husband] good and not evil all the days of her life." In Titus 2 Paul says women are "to love their husbands, to love their children, to be discreet, chaste, homemakers, good, obedient to their own husbands, that the word of God may not be blasphemed" (vv. 4b-5).

Those in authority (Titus 3:1). God's Word tells us to "be subject to rulers and authorities, to obey, to be ready for every good work."

The lost and the saved (Gal. 6:9-10). Instruction is given to Christians to "do good to all, especially to those who are of the household of faith." Yes, we are to be "do gooders" in the right sense of the word. Ours is to be a life of good works.

BIBLICAL WOMEN OF GOOD WORKS

In addition to the Proverbs 31 woman, there are so many other examples of women in the Bible who got it right in the good works department. Here are but a few:

◇ Dorcas was a seamstress who was full of good works (Acts 9:36-41).

◇ Phoebe was a "helper of many" (Rom. 16:1-2).

◇ Priscilla was called a fellow worker in Jesus Christ (Rom. 16:3-4).

◇ Mary "labored much for us [the apostles]" (Rom. 16:6).

◇ The women who came with Jesus from Galilee prepared His body and told of His resurrection (Luke 23:55—24:10).

With so great an example laid out for us, and with so great a cloud of witnesses cheering us on (Heb. 12:1), how can we do any less in the name of the God who has given us such immeasurably good gifts?

THE MINISTRY OF THE MUNDANE

God calls some to places of service that put them in front of people—in the limelight. But many He beckons to the ministry of the mundane. He needs those who will be willing to care for the sick, sweep the church, care for children in the nursery, cook and serve meals, clean house, and do the grocery shopping. God has a job for each of us to do, and we each need one another. As in our physical bodies, some members of Christ's body have a more significant, noticeable job, but each and every member has his or her function and vitally needs the others.

There are creative opportunities for ministry in small things as well as in large. Here are some examples our family has participated in. I'd encourage you to try one of these activities or to create one of your own.

Parents. At Christmas give your parents a different candle for each week in December with Scripture verses about light.

Widows. Have a special "party" for some of the widows in your church and share how Christ is a husband to the widow. My daughter Janice cross-stitched this Scripture verse for a widow in our church: "Weeping may endure for a night, but joy comes in the morning" (Ps. 30:5b).

Significant times. Make a Scripture book at a special occasion (birth of a baby, graduation, sickness). Handwrite Scripture verses pertaining to this event on 3 x 5 cards in a little spiral book. I made one on *deliverance* for my daughter to take to the delivery room when she was going to have a baby. I made one on *guidance* for my daddy when he needed direction about a move when he was very ill. I made one on *comfort* when my daughter Gayle had a miscarriage. One was on *strength* for someone else going through a great time of trouble. Another was on *hope and joy* for someone who had come out of a great struggle into great joy. Most recently I made one for my husband about *the heart* when he was recovering from heart surgery.

Loss of a loved one. I made a cassette tape, reading Scriptures and singing songs about heaven and telling of the glories of that wonderful place and sent them to my oldest granddaughter, Renae, when her Grammy Bradley died.

Ministry to my children and grandchildren. I can accomplish this goal in numerous small and seemingly insignificant acts. One day on a walk I found a beautiful bird's feather and sent it to my missionary grandson Jonathan in Spain. He was around three years old at the time. He is fifteen now. In these years I have sent him feathers from all around the world. It is exciting to find a feather—for it makes me think of Jonathan. It is our special thing.

I have left a candle burning in the window, waiting the arrival of my then college-age son, David. I have put up a big "Welcome Home" sign for a returning child. On a stop traveling through the North Carolina mountains, my husband and I bought three beautiful rocks apiece for each of our grandsons. We enjoyed picking them out. Each of these examples represents just a small thing—or does it?

THIS BEARS MY LOVE

A number of years ago on Valentine's Day, my husband gave me a small stuffed bear holding a heart that said, "This bears my love." It has been all over the world. It has now become a tradition between us to try to surprise the other person in the most unusual and creative place with our "love bear."

This little bear has shown up in the refrigerator, the cereal box, in a shoe, in a suitcase, and many other places. On Father's Day one year I asked our minister of music to give the "love bear" to my preacher husband during the time of the service when everyone was shaking hands. No one but Adrian and I and the minister of music knew our little secret. But it was special.

I must confess that Adrian has topped them all with two unexpected arrivals of the "love bear." One was when we were eating dinner in a hotel on the Mount of Olives in Jerusalem. Everyone else had been served, and I had nothing to eat. Then the waiter finally brought in my meal, covered with a special silver dome. When he lifted it off, there was the "love bear." Adrian had brought it all the way to Israel. Was I ever surprised and delighted. (I did eventually get my dinner served—but this was a far better gift.)

The one that tops them all was when we were to have a special protocol visit with the vice mayor of Moscow in his opulent office. Pictures were being made after the meeting, and I was taking videos. Then the vice-mayor walked from the other side of the room over to me and handed me—would you believe—the "love bear." He did not speak English, but my husband had told him through an interpreter that he wanted him to help play a joke on me. He did not completely understand our little joke, but I thought it was so funny that I broke out laughing.

Yes, we had taken something more profound with us on that trip. We had taken a selection of ten outstanding Christian books written in Russian, including a Bible, C. S. Lewis's *Mere Christianity*, James Dobson's *Dare to Discipline*, and others to give to the mayor (who was out of town), the vice-mayor, and half a dozen of their deputies. Above all, we had taken our love and our witness for Jesus Christ. But perhaps even the "love bear" had a part in our ministry that day.

Indeed, it is fun to be creative in little acts of love and kindness as well as in big things.

GOD'S WORD LIKE A MIRROR

James tells us, "But be doers of the word, and not hearers only, deceiving yourselves" (James 1:22). If we are just hearers, we are like a woman who took a look at herself in the mirror and saw that she needed to wash her face and curl and brush her hair. But she did not pay attention to what the mirror "told" her and took no action on what she saw—promptly forgetting it all together. God wants us to take a look in His Book, pay attention, and be doers and not just hearers. Then we will be blessed.

The author of Hebrews prays a blessing on those who have been saved through the blood of the covenant. It includes a perfecting "in every good work to do His will." I offer it today as a prayer and a benediction for you, my dear reader: "Now may the God of peace who brought up our Lord Jesus from the dead, that great Shepherd of the sheep, through the blood of the everlasting covenant, make you complete in every good work to do His will, working in you what is well pleasing in His sight, through Jesus Christ, to whom be glory forever and ever. Amen" (Heb. 13:20-21).

PRACTICING THE PROMISES

Lord, I WILL . . .

◇ Choose a good name over fame and riches.

◇ Express my appreciation to my parents for areas in which they have been a good example to me.

◇ Make things right with anyone I have personally wronged.

◇ Exchange my sins for His goodness.

◇ Make it a habit to "abide in Christ" in every circumstance of my life, whether good or so-called bad.

◇ Do something good this week (call, visit, send a card, etc.) for a widow or someone in need.

◇ Think of someone who has been a blessing to me and call and tell the person about it.

8

A Good Land

The Result of Our Leaning on Jesus

~ ~

Thousands of years ago, God promised to Abraham a good land. It was called Canaan because the Canaanites had previously occupied it. Because of God's promise to His chosen people, it became known as the Promised Land.

When it came time for Abraham's descendants to possess the land, God made these promises to Moses and the people: "For the LORD your God is bringing you into a good land" (Deut. 8:7a); "a land flowing with milk and honey" (Deut. 6:3b). He would bring them from slavery in Egypt to freedom in Canaan. He would do the bringing, and He would do the preparing of the land to receive them. All they needed to do was obey and lean on Him—and watch Him work miracle upon miracle to fulfill His promise to them.

The journey from Egypt to Canaan pictures our journey from a sinful lifestyle to Spirit-filled living. Egypt stands for our life before we were saved. We were enslaved by sin as the children of Israel were enslaved. Pharaoh illustrates our hard taskmaster, Satan, who does not want to let us go.

The Passover Lamb points to Jesus Christ, who was our substitute—the sacrifice who took our place so that we would not have to die for our sins. God said, "When I see the blood, I will pass over you." Every family had to slay a lamb and put the blood on the doorpost; then each person within that house would be saved. Likewise, each one of us must choose to trust Jesus Christ to be our Passover Lamb.

Crossing the Red Sea represents stepping out by faith to cross over from Egypt to Canaan. We have to take that first step by faith before God miraculously opens our Red Sea and allows us to go over on dry land.

The good land of Canaan speaks of the Spirit-filled life. It was a land flowing with milk and honey and good fruit of all kinds. These are illustrations of the fruit of the Spirit—love, joy, peace, and the rest. God wants us to experience a brand-new day, claiming our Canaan—just as He wanted the Israelites to claim Canaan land right away instead of wandering through the desert for forty years. All along the hot, tiresome journey through the wilderness, just after crossing the Red Sea, the people learned under Moses' direction to lean on Jehovah God. And it was the picture of the Promised Land that kept the people hoping, dreaming of the day, keeping on keeping on.

It was only a short seven-day journey into Canaan, but God arranged a testing of their faith. Moses sent out twelve spies; they all brought back a report of what a good land it was. The country was abundant in provisions—a land flowing with milk and honey. But there was an obstacle; there were giants in the land. Yet ten of the spies hadn't learned to lean on God. They were frightened and forgot God's promise to be with them. The majority of the Israelites also failed to believe God. As a result many died in the wilderness. The others wandered in the wilderness for forty years. Only two of the spies, Joshua and Caleb, believed that the God upon whom they depended was able to give them the land. And only those two spies got to enter the land. There were many battles to be fought, but as long as they trusted God, they conquered.

Are you like the ten spies? Have you spied out the land, the land of the Spirit-filled life and seen the sweet fruit of the Spirit—love, joy, peace, and all the rest? Did you see a life of victory and joy, but you brought back an evil report of giants in this land—doubt and fear, hatred and strife? You would like that sweet fruit, but you're not able to defeat the giants.

We too can enter and claim *our* Canaan. We can win the many spiritual battles that lie ahead, if we believe that our great God will deliver us. However, many wander in a spiritual wilderness, failing to eat of the spiritual fruit of Canaan. God indeed has a good land of spiritual provisions for us if we will but follow and obey.

Many obstacles lie along the way. The giants of fear, selfishness, prayerlessness, doubt, and many others lurk in the shadows, prepared to defeat us along our journey to our Canaan. But God has promised us a land of Spirit-filled living if we but believe that He is a God "who is able."

So what about you? Are you a Caleb, a Joshua, who, though they knew the giants waited, believed that their God was able? Are you ready to lean on Him, abide in Him, and in Him possess the land of promise?

Claiming Our Canaan

It's a brand-new day claiming our Canaan.
It's a brand-new day trusting our Lord.
Onward to victory possessing the land,
Proving His Word while holding His hand.

J R

A TRIP TO THIS GOOD LAND

I have read about this good land since I was a little girl. I was acquainted with the names of many places in this country and of many people who had walked the paths of this Promised Land.

When I was thirty-seven years old, I made a trip to the Holy Land for the first time. It was exciting to experience the places with which I had been familiar since my youth. It was like meeting "old friends" but seeing them for the first time.

My husband and I now have led groups to this land many times. I have never tired of seeing this holy place and experiencing firsthand the fulfillment of God's promises to Israel. And in this land on my many visits I've seen an up-close, new vision of what it means to lean on Jesus—in the nitty gritty of a dangerous existence.

Since Abraham's temporary lapse in faith that produced Ishmael, warfare has existed between the Arabs and the Jews. This strife is greatly evidenced in the land today. In fact, the whole world has been in turmoil and has been riddled with terrorism because of this tremendous conflict.

My husband and I have become personally acquainted with both Jews and Arabs. We have come to see that there are indeed two sides to the problems in this land. Perhaps in the stories of two of our dear friends (one on each side of the ethnic conflict), you'll see illustrated more clearly than ever the dichotomy of God's promise of a good land and the danger inherent in leaning on Him through the journey to get there.

MIRIAM FINDS FREEDOM

I will never forget a young Jewish woman called Miriam who was our guide over thirty years ago. She was a real patriot. She had been among those who had escaped Nazi Germany and was among the first to land secretively on the shores of Israel after its independence was declared on May 14, 1948. She loved this good land. To her it represented freedom and a new beginning.

I can see her now in my memory—a lovely Jewish woman, so open, so warm, so willing to build a bridge of understanding between us who were so different. She a Jew—I a Christian.

She fled for her life from persecution in Germany; I came from a land of freedom, a land I have taken too much for granted. We met in Israel, God's miracle land. She was our guide. Six days with Miriam. I never dreamed you could learn to love in so short a time. I never knew I could love someone of another race, another religion like this. From half a world away—why this strange bond?

The answer lies, I'm sure, in the mystery of the Promised Land. I too "love" the Land of Israel, although from a different perspective than hers.

She knew and felt something I could not know. But I comprehended things that her eyes could not see. And in those days we unveiled some secrets to each other. She held a Torah in her hand and shared the value of this book. At the Western Wall on the Sabbath she told how the people came to pray for their Messiah. She showed us the cup that was used at Passover for the Guest who was always welcome to come.

She shared from her heart and with her lovely voice the songs of Israel. As I caught the spirit of these people, I joined with her to sing "Next Year in Jerusalem." I, too, wanted to return next year.

She and her husband had sought refuge there since Israel had become a nation. She had lived in fear—with machine gun in hand.

Courage and patriotism were surging through her. She loved this land. How proud she was of it.

She had seen God work miracles of deliverance for her people; she believed Israel belonged to the Jews—the Jews of all the world. They would make room for all the persecuted, forsaken, homesick Jews. All who came would be a part of the nation.

When she came to Israel, she wanted a new life, a new beginning, even a new name. She would choose her own—it would be *Miriam*. What better namesake than the sister of Moses, the great leader of deliverance.

We learned from her, but she listened to us, too—to the songs we sang, to the messages preached, to the love we shared in our group, to the testimonies of transformed lives. And I know she heard one sermon if nothing else—the one that said for six days, "We love you, Miriam"; for we did love her. We told her and showed her.

I know she heard because as the last day was coming to an end and she was saying farewell, her voice broke; her eyes brimmed with tears. Yes, she loved us, too.

It was the Savior's love that wove our hearts together. He used different colored threads—some cheerful, some somber. He used the thread of love for God's chosen people, for their beloved land of Israel, for the holy city of Jerusalem. He used the thread of knowledge of the Scriptures—both hers and ours, the Old and New together. He used the thread of mutual old-time friends— these familiar places I had known for years through the pages of the Bible, the cities that Jesus knew, lakes he sailed, mountains and rugged paths He climbed. Miriam knew these friends as well; she had seen these places, crossed the lakes, and walked the hills and valleys. I knew them with my heart and mind—she with her eyes and feet and heart.

She introduced us to these mutual old-time friends for the first time, face to face. She lived and worked in this land that I, too, had "known" since childhood. It was so mysterious—this common bond that drew our hearts together.

Miriam

We love
your smile,
your song,
your openness,
your patriotism,
your courage,
your understanding.
But most of all
we love you.

Oh, how I pray that we will meet again—
in the Land of endless day,
in the Land where there'll be
no Jew nor Gentile;
where we will all be one "in Christ;"
in the Land where there will be
no war,
no tanks,
no bombs,
no guerrillas;
no sickness,
no suffering,
no sorrow,
no death.

In the Land where truly flows
abundant milk and honey,
in the Land where Jesus is the Light—
where there will be no darkness at all!
Miriam, will we meet again?
Please meet me just inside the Eastern Gate.

In Christ We Love Both Jew and Arab

Yes, we love Miriam and her people. But in Christ we love both Jew and Arab. We believe that God loves the Jew and promised this good land to Israel forever. But God also loves the Arab. We have good friends who are Christian Arabs. Philip Saad pastors a Christian Arab church in Haifa, Israel.

We have also had Arab guides. We have traveled with a Christian Arab Tour company many times. The Arab guide who has captivated our hearts and shown us the "other side" is named Saad Shaar. He pastors a Christian Arab church in Haifa, Israel. Late one evening Saad showed my husband a scar left by an Israeli soldier's bayonet when Saad was a little boy.

Saad shared how difficult it was to overcome the hatred he had for the Jewish people. My husband responded that it was only through the Holy Spirit that he could find the power to love his enemies. Saad, like Miriam, was our guide for six days in Israel. His name meant happy, but he seemed so sad.

Born in the country he calls Palestine, his home is Jerusalem—the city of the King. We were a group from Tennessee, come to see the Land of the Bible—the land we had read about since childhood. He had been here before Israel became a nation; to him this was the land of *his* people—the Palestinians.

For years they had sowed their seed, winnowed their wheat, shepherded their flocks, baked their bread, picked their grapes, and eaten their yogurt and cheese. They lived in their tents and houses, owned businesses, and sold their wares. To them it was a good land, even though many lived in the desert, rode their donkeys, and worked with homemade tools. The land gave them their lives.

Saad lived just outside the ancient city wall of Jerusalem. His family was well respected. He had no concerns as a little boy except to run and play, to observe and learn all that his active mind could absorb.

But one day fear filled his little heart. War broke out, and his life fell apart when both father and mother were killed. When only six, he saw his dear mother shot. Later a twin brother died in prison. Saad was too young to understand—but not too young to hate. His life was filled with quiet desperation, his family scattered, his goals blocked at every turn. He was a man without a country. "They" had taken his away. He was feared and mistrusted by many, ready at any time to restore the land to his people.

But Saad was man of truth and accuracy, a man who thirsted after knowledge—the likes of which we had rarely seen. He knew much about this land, from Dan to Beersheba—the desert land of the Bedouins, the waterfalls and brooks of the north, the fertile Jordan valley, and the mountains round about Jerusalem.

We were sent on a mission. We thought it was a trip, but our mission truly was to give and receive love. True love—that only God can give; expressed through word and song, kisses and embraces, and tear-brimmed eyes.

In time, Saad became a Christian through my husband's witness. My husband had spent many late hours encouraging him to allow Jesus to heal his heart and remove the hatred he held for the Israelis who had hurt his family.

Saad told us we were dearer than friends, closer than brothers and sisters. He said our love for each other—his and ours—was as high as the stars, as spacious as the skies, as deep as the ocean. How did we come to love Saad so soon? The love of God in our hearts touched his heart, and his heart reached out to us.

Saad

Jesus is the only One
Who can heal the brokenhearted;
Jesus is the only One
Who can love your enemies through you;
Jesus is the only One
Who can restore that which has been taken away.

To hate is to make war;
Through Him we learn to love;
To sin is to make evil;
Through Him we are made righteous.

Love and righteousness make peace;
He truly is our peace—
To possess Him is to possess peace,
For He is the Prince of Peace.

JESUS, THE ONLY ANSWER TO THIS AGE-OLD PROBLEM

Many years have come and gone since we met Miriam and Saad. Even though I never forgot Miriam, I lost track of her because we developed a long-term relationship with the Christian Arab Tour company where we met Saad.

Over twenty years after Miriam first guided us, I was updating my Christmas card list and ran across her name and address. I added her to my list. Imagine my surprise and great delight when one day after Christmas a card arrived from her. It said she had been listening to Adrian in Naharia (Israel) on our "Love Worth Finding" broadcast over Mid-Eastern Television.

I knew I must see Miriam again. God had put a love for her in my heart many years before that had never died. On our next trip to Israel we invited her and her husband to have dinner with us and our group at our hotel at the Sea of Galilee, just a couple of hours from where she lived.

When I had last seen her, we both had wept when we said good-bye. But would she have a similar feeling all these years later? It was a memorable moment when we met. We were both twenty years older, but the memories flooded my soul as we embraced. Yes, she too remembered.

We asked her to share her dramatic story with our group. Saad was also invited to this meeting, and I'm sure he felt a twinge over our obvious love for this Jewish woman. You see, our hearts were now also entwined with this Arab guide, who held no good feelings toward any Jew. His life and family had been torn to shreds by some Israelis, and forgiveness wouldn't come easily.

I knew that we must have Miriam guide us again, but there was no way that we could forsake Saad. In my heart God used these two to illustrate the conflict between the Israelis and the Palestinians. I knew also that Jesus is the only answer to this age-old problem.

God worked out a plan for Miriam to guide us for a couple of days in Jerusalem for our last several trips to Israel. In her lovely, warm, outgoing way, she has reached out to Saad. I have asked Saad to pray for Miriam, and by the Lord's help, Saad has reached back to her.

In recent days the Israeli/Palestinian conflict has intensified. A new level of terrorism has touched Israel through homicide bombers willing to take their own lives as they kill others. They are deceived into thinking that they are doing "God's will."

I frequently e-mail Miriam to keep up with her and to assure her of my love and prayers. Indeed, my love for her is a "God thing." She escaped the horror of the Holocaust as a child, but now she faces the hatred of terrorists.

We have talked on the phone to Saad. He is not guiding because few groups are going to Israel right now. He told my husband, "Thank you for teaching me about the Holy Spirit." Then he quoted the words to a song I usually sing when going through the area of Gilead. The song speaks of a balm in this land that makes the wounded whole. The verse ends:

> *There is a balm in Gilead*
> *To heal the sin-sick soul.*

I have encouraged Saad to use his great ability as a guide and teacher to be a peacemaker for Jesus. I sent him these words of encouragement, titled "He Is Our Peace."

He Is Our Peace

> *Though some cry peace, there is no peace;*
> *For they had no shame*
> *And knew not how to blush (Jer. 6:14-15);*
> *Everyone dealt falsely.*
> *They only cared about themselves (Jer. 6:13).*
>
> *Then Jesus came—the Prince of Peace;*
> *He is the Mighty God,*
> *The Everlasting Father (Isa. 9:6).*
> *The angels sang, "Glory to God and on earth,*
> *Peace, good will toward men!" (Luke 2:14).*
> *And He declared, "In Me you may have peace" (John 16:33).*
>
> *Still there's war and hatred on every hand*
> *In the city of our God—Jerusalem.*

In the so-called city of peace, there is no peace,
But fear and constant vigil.

Amidst the turmoil caused by
selfishness and pride,
Amidst division caused by race and nation
He came to make us one (Eph. 2:14).
He has broken down the wall between
Gentile and Jew;
So to create in Himself one new man from two
That He might reconcile both to God
in one body through the cross (Eph. 2:14-16).

For those who will confess that Jesus Christ is Lord,
Who will believe that God raised Him from the dead—
For those who ask Him
to rule within their hearts,
They may have this peace (Rom. 10:9-10).

Then one day—in His time
Peace will come on earth;
The lion and the lamb lie down together (Isa. 11:6-7);
Then the Prince of Peace will rule
There in Jerusalem—the city of our God (Rev. 20:4).
And there will be peace forevermore (Rev. 21:22—22:5).

PRACTICING THE PROMISES

Lord, I WILL . . .

◇ Read Deuteronomy 8 and circle the words *good* and *land*, reminding myself of God's good land that He provided to His ancient people and how it illustrates His provisions for me.

◇ Claim my own personal "Canaan" and enter into the land of Spirit-filled living.

◇ Recall aloud to someone else one of God's good gifts to me and what He taught me through it.

◇ Memorize Colossians 3:17 and endeavor to honor the Lord in all I do and say.

◇ Read Galatians 5:22-23 and memorize the nine fruits of the Spirit.

◇ Ask God to show me my areas of weakness and surrender to Him to fill me with his Holy Spirit.

9

Sharing His Goodness

Giving Others Someone to Lean Upon

~ ~

As we have reflected on God's great goodness, some of you have responded, "Oh, yes, I know the Good Shepherd. He has been right here with me, inviting me to lean upon Him in the darkest night. I have feasted at His banquet table even when my enemies were near. I have tasted His wonderful provisions. He has given me His righteousness in exchange for my sin. Yes, He has led me thus far, and I know He will lead me home. He is working all things together for good because I really do love Him and want to do His will."

That's terrific.

But there is another step in the leaning process. As we're learning to lean, we will begin to look a little like Him. And if we are to be like Jesus, we will become under-shepherds to the little flocks God gives to each of us. Remember, He gathers us like a shepherd. "He shall feed his flock like a shepherd: he shall gather the lambs with his arm, and carry them in his bosom, and shall gently lead those that are with young" (Isa. 40:11 KJV).

He will teach us to do the same. This is yet another lesson in leaning.

"I'LL EXPLAIN IT TO YOU LATER"

Our personal shepherding should begin with our own family. One of the sweetest examples I have seen of this was when I saw and heard my son shepherding his son. On two occasions I just "happened" to overhear and observe them. As I watched, what a blessing came to my own life.

The first occasion was during the serving of the Lord's Supper. My son David and his family, who are missionaries to Spain, were home on furlough and visiting our church. Little Jonathan, who was five years old at the time, was seated between his daddy and me. As the bread was passed, Jonathan began asking questions: "What is this, and what is it for?" Then the grape juice was served; and, of course, the same questions came pouring out. I heard my son patiently answer in the simplest way he could.

A couple of months later the identical situation occurred. Jonathan began to ask the same questions, and David whispered back, "I'll explain it to you later."

Later when Jonathan's mind was on other things, David had not forgotten. I was in the room when David called Jonathan over and lifted him up on his lap. He explained how the bread pictured the body of Jesus and the grape juice represented His blood. He then told Jonathan how Jesus had died in his place. I was so blessed to hear this private conversation.

"OH, MAMA, I'M SO GLAD YOU'RE PREGNANT!"

About a year later I went to Spain to visit David, Kelly, and Jonathan. Kelly was two months pregnant. They were all thrilled. Jonathan, now six years old, patted his mama on the stomach and said, "Oh, Mama, I'm so glad you're pregnant."

The day I arrived, Kelly began to have a problem with her

pregnancy. A week later, on my birthday, she miscarried. That morning I was putting breakfast on the table. David came into the room and told me that he was getting ready to take Kelly to the hospital.

At that moment Jonathan walked into the room. He asked if something was wrong. David then invited him to sit in his lap. He then proceeded to tell him in the most gentle, tender way that the baby was going to die.

I was so touched by David's gentleness as he gathered his "little lamb" to himself to share their heartbreak. Again I had been privileged to see and hear my son feed his son spiritually, gently like a shepherd.

No *Niño*

Kelly and David then left for the hospital. Jonathan and I stayed home and waited. After a while the phone rang. I answered and didn't recognize the caller's voice—or her language. I tried the few Spanish words I knew—hospital, Kelly, no *niño*, which meant that Kelly was in the hospital and that there was no baby. Then the caller began to speak Spanish very fast, and I could not understand what she was saying.

The next time the phone rang, I decided to let Jonathan, who is bilingual, answer. He calmly talked to the caller and then hung up. I asked, "Jonathan, what did they want?" He said that they had asked how his mommy was. I asked, "What did you say?"

He calmly replied, "I told them the baby died." It was all that I could do to fight back the tears. *Oh, God, please help me to say and do what would be helpful to Jonathan.*

God was so real to us all day. He gave me a great peace and comfort to share with Jonathan. We played and we prayed. Several times we talked to Mimi (the other grandmother) and the two grandfathers back in the United States; then we talked to God. We read books and watched children's videos; we read God's Word; David called and talked to Jonathan. God got us through that long day as we combined the mundane and the profound of life.

That evening when David and Kelly arrived home around 8 P.M., I could not believe what they had brought with them. They came in the door apologizing about my birthday and carrying a "birthday pie." "A pie was all that we could find," they said. David then gave me a necklace he had bought. Tears came to my eyes as I realized that in their grief they had thought of me.

MY SHEPHERD SON

Indeed, what a shepherd my son is. At that time he was the pastor of a little flock of Spanish believers in Badajoz, Spain. He is also the leader of his family, which at that moment included me. But Jesus is the Chief Shepherd, watching over David and all of us—guiding and equipping us to lift up the fallen and to restore broken souls.

The next morning when I awoke, I heard my shepherd-son singing to the Lord although his heart was greatly saddened. I knew all was well—well with his soul.

It is more than two years later, and the Good Shepherd has guided. He has fulfilled a dream, and there is another *niño* in the Rogers's household, little Stephen Paul. Praise the Lord. God is so good—all the time.

"FEED MY SHEEP"

Yes, your flock begins with your own family. Then it reaches out to your neighbors and friends, extends to the bag boy at the grocery store, the shoe repair man, the waitress at the restaurant, the person who sits beside you on the airplane, the woman who styles your hair, the plumber who fixes your kitchen sink.

Jesus said, "And other sheep I have which are not of this fold; them also I must bring, and they will hear My voice; and there will be one flock and one shepherd" (John 10:16). Jesus also said to Peter that memorable morning on the shore of Galilee, "Simon, son of Jonah, do you love Me? . . . Feed My sheep" (John 21:16-17).

After he had shown the disciples His hands and His side, Jesus said to them, "Peace to you! As the Father has sent Me, I also send you" (John 20:21). He has commanded us to go and make disciples.

Yes, wherever you go, God wants you to reach out and touch those in your world with His love and the good news of Jesus Christ. If you are following the Good Shepherd, He will lead and guide you to others who need Him. He will lead us all into His one fold.

Many years ago I stood at a graveside and said good-bye to a precious baby boy. My heart was broken, and the tears overflowed, but God did graciously bring healing to my life. He gave me a song to sing and a desire to reach out and touch the grieving, hurting hearts in my world for Christ.

Yes, God has worked this heartache and many others together for good. When Christ has touched your life and brought peace to your storm, you do not worry about what you will say when you find yourself in someone else's storm. You just want to reach out and touch them with the healing power of Christ.

Some years ago two tragedies occurred in one week among our church family. I was there on both occasions during the intensity of their grief. We arrived at the hospital right after Lily and Ted had heard that their precious two-year-old daughter Joy had died after being run over by a car. I moved over and put my arms around the young mother and just held her as her body shook like a leaf. Lily needed my touch just then. Perhaps because I'd been through my own times of leaning, I knew intuitively what this young mother most craved.

We arrived at the other home just after a father had told his three grief-stricken children that their mother had been murdered. I reached out to touch and hold those children. Then I sat for a while and wept with them. God wants you and me to be available to reach out with the healing power of Jesus Christ and touch those in our world who are hurting. He'll show you what to do and what to say; but we must go, and we must go now.

WHAT CAN I DO? WHAT CAN YOU DO?

Several years ago my brother Curtis developed a malignant tumor and had to have his eye removed. They thought they got all of the cancer. When I went to visit him, he gave me a little hour glass—or I should say a little "moment glass." On one end he had engraved these words: "Only one life—shall soon be past; only what's done for Jesus will last." On the other end of the glass was this quote from Psalm 31:15: "My times are in Your hand."

A year later the cancer returned. Within three weeks he was with Jesus. I keep this little "moment glass" on a shelf in my kitchen to remind me that we only have *this* moment; the next is not guaranteed.

How often have I procrastinated? How often have you waited until later, and the opportunity was gone? We only have this moment to reach out and touch our world for Christ.

What will I do with this moment? When my children were small, I had that moment to lead them to Christ and to teach them to reach out to others in their world. Since God healed my broken heart, He has sent me time and time again to help in comforting other broken hearts. Only God can take heartache and pain and work it *together for good.*

I have an empty nest now. What can I do? What can you do? We can take whatever we have that God has worked together for good in our lives and reach out and touch those in our hurting world for Christ.

God wants you and me to be available to reach out and touch those in our world with the healing power of Jesus Christ. He'll show you what to do and what to say. But we must go, and we must go now.

PRACTICING THE PROMISES

Lord, I WILL . . .

◇ Take the good and so-called bad that God has allowed in my life and share what God has taught me with someone else I know and love.

◇ Gather my children like little lambs and teach them to love and trust Jesus.

◇ Shepherd the flock that God has given to me, whether small or large.

◇ Take this moment and reach out and touch the life of someone in my world with God's love and the good news of Jesus Christ.

◇ Consider the claims of the gospel and make sure that I am saved.

◇ Tell someone this Christmas that "He was born to die."

◇ Tell someone this coming Easter that "Christ is risen."

10

Giving Out of Our Weakness

Leaning When We Don't Understand

～～

Let me share the story of some people God brought into my life to join the team of shepherding others—people I didn't even realize were on the team, but people who have blessed me as I watched them show others how to lean on Jesus. As we reached out together to touch a hurting family with God's love, God reached back to each of us with His love and blessings—individually and corporately. May they encourage you to reach out and touch the people in your world—now, before it is too late.

OVERWHELMED

I had not seen Ernie for years. She was in the hospital awaiting surgery for a tumor on her pancreas. I went immediately when I found out. Sensing that she wanted to talk about her relationship with the Lord, I turned to my favorite chapter in the Bible, Psalm 18. I read verse 1, which says, "I will love You, O LORD, my strength."

I challenged her to be like David and to declare her love for Jesus Christ and to trust Him regardless of the outcome. She said she wanted to do this. So we prayed and committed her future to our great God. This seemed to bring her peace.

The next day I was with the family when the doctor brought the news that the tumor was inoperable. We wept and prayed together and asked God for help to face the future. This began a five-month walk through "the valley of the shadow of death" with Ernie and her family.

When I left the hospital that day, I told the Lord that I was overwhelmed with His assignment to me. The next week *I* was to have surgery. Three weeks after that our daughter was getting married in our home. Then a week later we were going to see our missionary son in Spain. On and on my schedule went.

I would have said I could not do this, but God said to my heart—much louder than words, "This one is yours—shepherd her." I then prayed, "Lord, either send someone to help, or make it possible for me to minister to this family." Well, God did provide unique and timely answers to both prayers—although I didn't always know or recognize what He had in mind until after the fact.

Through those months Ernie's twin sister, Katie, and Katie's husband, Alan, came to know Christ and were baptized. They all came to church the two following Sundays. Then Ernie got worse. They called for me to come. It was the last time I talked to her.

The family was gathered around her bed. Ernie said, "I'm ready to die. Will you pray that God will take me tonight?" I've never been asked something like that before. But I thanked the Lord that Ernie was trusting Him. I told Him that Ernie was ready, and asked Him, if it was His will, would He take her on home? Ernie went home to be with Jesus the next day.

NOT THE END, ONLY THE BEGINNING

This is not the end of the story but rather the beginning. Yes, Ernie's physical life has ended but not her influence. She had taken her last moments to urge her family to be faithful to church and Sunday school. Some of them have been there faithfully since then. Ernie's life with Jesus continues on. She now sees face to face the One for whom she had declared her love. Life eternal has begun for others who now have the assurance that they will see Jesus and Ernie face to face one day (1 Cor. 13:12). And my life will never be the same.

I thank Him for my "walk through the valley" with Ernie. It has reminded me of the true values and priorities of life. God can enable me to take the moment I have to touch someone in my world for my Savior.

Although Ernie has gone home, I have made lifelong friends of other family members. You can't "walk through the valley of the shadow of death" without getting close to those who walk with you.

ON THE TEAM

One of the many lessons I learned through this experience is that God has many others who are "on the team" leading His chosen ones to Himself. At first I thought I was all alone in ministering to this family. I was overwhelmed with what I perceived to be God's assignment.

Sometime after that first visit in the hospital, the Lord began to show me the other helpers "on the team." I have named it "team witnessing." There was Alan's daughter Jamie, whom I met and prayed with over the phone. Then there was Katie's dentist. While she was in his dentist chair, he asked her if she was sure that she

133

was saved, and he prayed with her right there. There was my husband, who prayed with Alan to receive Christ.

At the funeral I saw Mathel, who worked with Ernie at her beauty parlor and had talked to Ernie about the Lord. Mathel asked me, "Do you think Ernie was saved?" And I was able to say, "Praise God, she was." Then at the graveside I saw Candy, a friend of Ernie's daughter Cindy. Candy had given Cindy a Bible.

As I was standing there talking to Jamie, it suddenly dawned on me that we were all on the team—all part of God's team leading Ernie and her family members to Jesus Christ. I said to Jamie, "Let me introduce you to Candy, a member of 'the team.'" No telling how many others were on this team—members we had never met. Someday we'll have a grand team reunion in heaven!

I just have to say, "Thank You, Lord, for this mission impossible. For with You, all things are possible. Your promises are true. No, I don't understand all the pain and suffering, but I know that 'all things work together for good to those who love God, to those who are the called according to His purpose.'"

Will you begin now to reach out to those in your world with the healing touch of Jesus Christ? Remember, most often in our world He chooses to use no hands but our hands.

PRACTICING THE PROMISES

Lord, I WILL . . .

◇ Live as if Jesus is coming back at any moment.

◇ Reflect again on the unfailing promises of the Twenty-third Psalm and the magnificent assurance of Romans 8:28 and ask myself, "Is Jesus my Good Shepherd? Am I following Him?"

◇ Pray diligently that the Lord will use my gifts, my abilities, my history of pain and restoration to minister to someone else who is hurting.

◇ Ask God for His strength and His wisdom in shepherding the flocks He entrusts to my care—and for the willingness to seize each moment today to care for these loved ones.

11

Peace in the Storm

The Ultimate Result of Leaning Hard on Jesus

~ ~

Many of the unpleasant consequences of our choices can be explained and definitely are deserved. But away with all pious platitudes spoken by those who have never walked the shadowy path of the unexplainable and have never pondered the depths of undeserved consequences.

Have you cried out, "My God, my God, why have You forsaken me?" Circumstances did not work out the way you wanted. God did not answer your prayers exactly as you wished. Simple principles and formulas did not work the way you thought they would. Somehow you were the exception to the rule. Did that mean that God did not hear you when you cried to Him? Does it mean He doesn't care? Oh no; that is not true at all.

Jesus understands those who are forsaken. Isaiah tells us, "'For the LORD has called you like a woman forsaken and grieved in spirit, like a youthful wife when you were refused'" (Isa. 54:6). He points out the good: "'For a mere moment I have forsaken you . . . but with everlasting kindness I will have mercy on you,' says the LORD, your Redeemer" (Isa. 54:7-8).

I CANNOT TELL YOU WHY

No, I cannot tell you why some people die suddenly without warning. No, I cannot tell you why some suffer terribly with horrible diseases. I do not know why a man forsakes his wife and the children who love him. I do not know why some exist in a coma for years. I do not know why hundreds of people die in a plane crash or why thousands die in a terrorist attack. I do not know why some couples who want children desperately can't have them and why some women kill their unborn infants.

I don't know why, why, why some people are plagued with tragedy and others suffer little in this life. But I know, I know, I know that "all things work together for good to those who love God, to those who are the called according to His purpose" (Rom. 8:28). And I know this: To all those who lean on Him, God offers peace in the midst of every storm.

God never explained the why of the circumstances, but He gave a magnificent assurance of all things working together for good. Life may seem like an earthquake, perhaps 7.5 on the Richter scale. "For the mountains shall depart and the hills be removed" (Isa. 54:10a), but the good (oh, so good) is, "'My kindness shall not depart from you, nor shall My covenant of peace be removed,' says the Lord who has mercy on you" (Isa. 54:10b).

Did you know that God provides a multitude of mercies? But the children of Israel did not remember these mercies (Ps. 106:7). They provoked God at the Red Sea. When the seemingly impossible arose, they complained. They forgot the mercies of God. They did not even remember God's great deliverance from Egypt. When unpredictable problems come our way, will we forget God's mercies? Will we forget all our lessons and refuse to lean on His ever-present arm?

His Covenant of Peace

In our stunted way of thinking we imagine we will escape the trials and traumas of life, but God never promised a trouble-free life. Nevertheless, God has promised peace. He said that His promise, His covenant of peace with us, would not be removed (Isa. 54:10).

Jesus reaffirmed this covenant: "Peace I leave with you, My peace I give to you; not as the world gives do I give to you. Let not your heart be troubled, neither let it be afraid" (John 14:27). Peace is not only promised for ourselves, but assured to our children if we but claim it. "All your children shall be taught by the LORD, and great shall be the peace of your children" (Isa. 54:13).

Who will receive comfort and God's multitude of mercies? Who knows this peace that passes understanding? All those who take the risk and lean on Him. Listen to His promise: "O you afflicted one, tossed with tempest, and not comforted, behold, I will lay your stones with colorful gems, and lay your foundations with sapphires. I will make your pinnacles of rubies, your gates of crystal, and all your walls of precious stones" (Isa. 54:11-12).

What beautiful jewels will be given to this one so fair, this one who is being made into His image. God declares that in that day when He makes up His jewels, they shall be His (Mal. 3:17). We will be His jewels and will be given His jewels. How precious we are to Him, our heavenly Bridegroom.

Tossed with the Tempest

I do not tell you something I know nothing about. I have been tossed with the tempest. I have almost gone under the monstrous waves, but He at that very last moment, when His hand was all I had to cling to, whispered, "Peace, be still." He is a covenant-keeping God. He has not only brought me peace, but He has brought great peace to my children (Isa. 54:13). I have claimed this promise by faith. Yes, "He calms the storm, so that its waves are still" (Ps. 107:29).

Calm the Storm

Oh, Lord, if You rule
the raging of the sea,
You can calm this tempest
deep inside of me.

The waves rise up like
billows in my soul;
You still them so that
my spirit is made whole.

In the storms of life
I cry to You, my God,
"Calm the storm,
Still the waves;
Take me from
the waters."

Then I'm glad because
the storm is quiet;
You gently comfort, guide,
and lead me safely home.
(Taken from Psalms 18:16; 89:9; 107:25-30)
JR

TREASURE AMID THE FEARS IN DEEP WATERS

For a number of years my son Steve and his wife, Cindi, had encouraged me to go snorkeling with them. They had told me about the beautifully colored fish and sea animals that they had seen on the reefs in the Bahamas. Finally, I agreed. Cindi's mom and dad would also go along on the trip.

I prepared myself for my own search for the treasures of the deep. I purchased a special prescription face mask and snorkeling tube. My husband rented a house, and we arrived at Man-O-War Cay in the Bahamas.

It took some doing to get me there. I had never been attracted to this type of adventure for several reasons. I could not swim well; I could not see well without my glasses; and I had heard about the dangers of the deep—sharks, barracudas, octopuses, etc. Eventually, my family's report of the beauty and their encouragement to join them in the search for God's treasures in the sea was what challenged me to participate.

The first day I learned to breathe through the snorkeling tube in shallow water. I saw a few little fish, and to me that was exciting. I was ready for step two. I was taken by boat to a place that had some rocky areas near the shore. My husband stayed with me as we skimmed over a small reef. I saw a number of brightly colored fish—shimmering blue, yellow, and black.

The next day I went by boat a short distance into the ocean where several larger reefs were located. I was waiting for some of the others to get into the water and check everything. I still was hesitant about being in over my head.

It was then that someone yelled, "Shark!" Any anticipation I had faded, and my better senses told me not to go into the water. Those still in the boat assured me that it was a nurse shark and that it did not attack people and had a very small opening for a mouth.

My husband got out of the boat and was gliding over the reef. He came back and urged me to get into the water. He said the reef was beautiful and the fish were magnificent.

Right when I was convinced and had put one leg over the boat, someone closer yelled, "Shark!" I thought, *That's it! The dangers of the deep are just too much for me.* Someone said that this was also a nurse shark. In addition, my husband said that he would stay right by me. Besides, the boat would be just a few yards away.

I still cannot believe it, but I did get into the beautiful, clear aqua water to go on my search for the treasures of the deep. I stayed with Adrian, and he took me by the hand and led me over the reef. Indeed there were extravagantly colored tropical fish. Anemones waved at me as I glided by. It was magnificent.

It was then that I looked up to check the location of the boat. It had drifted about a hundred yards away. I panicked! I took off my mask and yelled, "Come back!" The boat quickly came to pick me up. Everyone said I had done well for my first adventure in water over my head. But fear had stopped me short. As I reminisced about the experience, I was glad I had made preparation and made the choice to get out of the boat despite the danger. And I filed the experience away in my memory, although my husband had encouraged me to write down my experience.

Two years later the ring of the telephone awakened us. It was a call from our son. He and his wife, Cindi, had just received news that her mother, who was only fifty-seven, had died in her sleep. There was no warning, no time for farewells or expressions of love. The last time we had all been together was in the Bahamas. We had seen many beautiful sights together and had had wonderful times of fellowship around June and Richard's dinner table.

June's death was the encouragement I needed to complete the story of the treasures of the deep. I began to see spiritual applications and parallels to our snorkeling experience. I had plunged into the deep waters of the ocean at the insistence of others. The spiritual parallel occurred when our family was plunged unexpectedly into the deep waters of sorrow at June's unexpected death. Tears have flooded our eyes, as grief has torn at our hearts. But this journey into the depths has also revealed numerous beautiful spiritual treasures of the deep.

First there was the sweet comfort and peace of the Holy Spirit that embraced us, like the soothing movement of the water lapping over our souls. Then like the brightly colored fish hiding in the crevices of the coral, there were unexpected surprises of joy through our teardrops. We found that our hearts could not be sad when we thought of June being face to face with Jesus. How our hearts leaped for joy when we thought of her experiencing the glories of heaven!

The shimmering schools of fish that swam by were like the sweet memories that kept passing by as we looked at pictures and recalled past vacations and events. We remembered the delicious meals she had cooked, the time we had waited together for the birth of our first grandchild Renae, the many crafts she had made and given away in Jesus' name, and the prayers she had prayed for her family and others.

One of the most beautiful treasures of the deep was the love communicated by spontaneous expressions of tenderness, like the anemones that waved as I passed by.

The assurance that June possessed eternal life through faith in Jesus Christ was like the broad coral reef—the great bedrock on the ocean floor. The greatest discovery in our deep water of sorrow was June's Bible. One by one we looked through its pages— so worn with many promises, dated with names written to the side.

I saw Cindi's and Steve's names written there. She and I had covenanted together to pray that our children would love Jesus more than anything. Then there was her son Richard's name. She had prayed him into God's kingdom. What a spiritual treasure!

This book told of Jesus Christ, her solid Rock and hope of eternal life for her and her loved ones.

To crown it all, there was the confidence that God was always there. This was illustrated in my ocean experience by my husband who swam beside me, by the air I breathed to sustain me under the water, and by those in the boat who were always standing ready to rescue me if I panicked.

Yes, I could see the magnificent treasures of the deep if I stayed afloat and kept on breathing through the snorkeling tube. But there was also the knowledge of the blue sky up above. I knew that below the surface in the deep waters was not my natural environment. This plunge was only temporary. I was made to walk on the land and breathe the air. But I am so grateful that He was there in the deep, enabling me to see below the surface in the deep waters His many unique and beautiful treasures.

Spiritually, as long as I by faith keep breathing in my Savior's wonderful life, as long as I am confident that He is by my side and is always near to rescue me, I can, without panic, experience the beauty of His spiritual treasures of the deep—comfort, joy, precious memories, tenderness, assurance of eternal life, and the reality of His presence.

And then we know that one day we will sit down in heaven with June and our Lord and reminisce about the treasures of the deep and reflect upon the glories of Paradise. These two experiences in the deep waters were yet another lesson in leaning hard on Jesus.

THE ULTIMATE GOOD

If you love God and are called according to His purpose, you can know, be assured that whatever heartache, whatever deep waters, whatever trial He leads you through—God will work it together for good as you take the risk of leaning on His everlasting arms. The ultimate good is that we will be made into His image. We will be like Him.

The old hymn by Thomas O. Chisholm may be the best prayer for the heart that longs to lean hard on Jesus in good times and bad times. Let me share it with you.

O to Be Like Thee!

O to be like Thee! Blessed Redeemer,
This is my constant longing and prayer;
Gladly I'll forfeit all of earth's treasures,
Jesus, Thy perfect likeness to wear.

O to be like Thee! full of compassion,
Loving, forgiving, tender and kind;
Helping the helpless, cheering the fainting,
Seeking the wand'ring sinner to find.

O to be like Thee! O to be like Thee,
Blessed Redeemer, pure as Thou art!
Come in Thy sweetness, come in Thy fullness—
Stamp Thine own image deep on my heart.
THOMAS O. CHISHOLM

I leave you now with this beautiful benediction written by a New Testament believer who obviously had learned to lean on Jesus. His words are as true now, two millennia later, as they were the day he penned them to the early church: "Now to Him who is able to keep you from stumbling, and to present you faultless before the presence of His glory with exceeding joy, to God our Savior, who alone is wise, be glory and majesty, dominion and power, both now and forever. Amen" (Jude 24-25).

PRACTICING THE PROMISES

Lord, I WILL . . .

◇ Reach out for Christ's hand whenever I feel the waves of life beginning to swell in my own heart.

◇ Sing aloud the words of Thomas Chisolm's song, "O to Be Like Thee," and make them my heart's prayer.

◇ Claim the promise of Isaiah 54:13 for all those in the little flock God has called me to shepherd.

◇ Bring all my "why" questions to God and trust Him to give answers in His time—whether while I live this life or after I cross over into eternity.

◇ Glory in the cross and that He shed His precious blood for me.

◇ Sing "Nothing but the Blood of Jesus" and say, "Thank You for dying for me."

Epilogue:
Have You Heard the
Good News?

An Invitation to You to Lean on Jesus

～ ～

We have reflected on God's magnificent assurance in Romans 8:28 that "all things work together for good," and His unfailing promise in Psalm 23 that His "goodness and mercy shall follow [us]." Some of you may realize that you do not know the Good Shepherd of Psalm 23 personally. You cannot say with David, "The LORD is *my* Shepherd."

If you do not "know His voice," then you do not belong to Him—and have no access to lean on Him. But I have good news for you. If you believe the gospel, He is willing to be your Good Shepherd. He will leave the ninety-nine sheep in the fold and come searching for you. Let me share with you the good news about Jesus so that you may have the great privilege of leaning hard on Jesus.

HAVE YOU HEARD THE GOOD NEWS?
JESUS DIED FOR YOU!

I am sure you will agree that the popular thing today is to tell abroad the bad news in our newspapers and news broadcasts. Good news has a low profile. Reporters look for conflict and crime. Truly, "bad news travels fast."

But God's Word says to proclaim the *good* news of salvation from day to day. The word *gospel* literally means "good news." The gospel has come to mean the good news of Jesus Christ. Simply stated: He died, He was buried, and He rose from the grave. And to top it all, He's coming back again.

What is good about a death? To human beings, death is the most fearful of all experiences. Its companions are suffering, sickness, disease, and sorrow.

There is a sting to death that is unequaled. All who have experienced it know what I mean. There is a feeling of helplessness that cries out, "There is no pain like this pain." Yes, death is our enemy, and we all will be its victims sooner or later, for "it is appointed for men to die once" (Heb. 9:27).

To us there is nothing good about death, but the Bible declared that Jesus' death was good news. His death was like no other. He willingly gave His life. He laid it down of Himself. "No one takes it from Me, but I lay it down of Myself" (John 10:18). His death was the purpose of His coming into this world. He was born to die.

The Bible says in Revelation 13:8 that He was "slain from the foundation of the world." You see, His death was a substitutionary death. The Scripture declares that "the soul who sins shall die" (Ezek. 18:4b). But He did not sin; so He did not have to die. He chose to die. He took our sins and piled them on Himself.

For there is a second death—far greater than the first. Jesus said, "And do not fear those who kill the body but cannot kill the soul. But rather fear Him who is able to destroy both soul and body in hell" (Matt. 10:28). He did not want us to experience this second death that was "prepared for the devil and his angels" (Matt. 25:41). So He took our place. He died physically so we would not have to die spiritually.

And that is good news. Have you heard the good news that Jesus died *for you?*

WHEN BLOODSHED IS GOOD NEWS

His death also was good news because of His blood that He shed. Now this is contrary to our feelings. We do not like the sight of blood. Some people even get nauseated or faint when they see it. Yet the Bible says in Leviticus 17:11a, "The life of the flesh is in the blood." Nourishment flows to our body through the blood. Poison is removed through the blood.

Spiritually, we receive nourishment through Jesus' blood. Jesus told His followers in John 6:53, "Most assuredly, I say to you, unless you eat the flesh of the Son of Man and drink His blood, you have no life in you." Many murmured and were offended because they were unspiritual and could not understand the spiritual intent. Jesus then explained, "The words that I speak to you are spirit, and they are life" (John 6:63b).

The whole sacrificial system of the Old Testament pointed to the shedding of Christ's blood on the cross. Hymn-writer Robert Lowry explained this most profoundly in his classic hymn "Nothing but the Blood":

> *What can wash away my sin?*
> *Nothing but the blood of Jesus;*

149

What can make me whole again?
Nothing but the blood of Jesus.
Oh, precious is the flow that makes me white as snow;
No other fount I know, nothing but the blood of Jesus.

To me His blood is not gory, but glory. It is so beautiful to those who have spiritual eyes to see. I love to sing, to praise, to teach about His precious blood. For "the blood of Jesus Christ His Son cleanses us from all sin" (1 John 1:7). His shed blood is "good news." Jesus' death, what His disciples thought to be the worst thing that could happen, worked together for the ultimate good—our salvation.

HAVE YOU HEARD THE GOOD NEWS? HE ROSE FROM THE GRAVE!

His death also was good news because it led to His resurrection. It proved that He held the keys to death and hell. He knew that on the third day He would rise from the dead. He even told His disciples, but they didn't understand those comforting words until after He rose, when they remembered His words (Luke 24:8). If they had listened, if they had believed, their hearts could have been filled with joy sooner, instead of with fear and hopelessness.

Robert Lowry wrote in the classic Easter hymn "Christ Arose:"

Up from the grave He arose
With a mighty triumph o'er His foes;
He arose a Victor from the dark domain,
And He lives forever with His saints to reign:
He arose! He arose!
Hallelujah! Christ arose!

His resurrection was necessary—yes, imperative. For it was the proof, the validation of all that He had said and done. It proved Him to be the Son of God (Rom. 1:4). The Jews sought a sign, but Jesus refused to give them a sign except the sign of Jonah: "For as Jonah was three days and three nights in the belly of the great fish, so will the Son of Man be three days and three nights in the heart of the earth" (Matt. 12:40).

The Jews tried to invalidate it. They had the Romans set a guard at the stone-sealed tomb. They remembered that He had said, "After three days I will rise" (Matt. 27:63b). But the guards were "scared to death" of the angels who rolled the stone away. "And the guards shook for fear of him, and became like dead men" (Matt. 28:4). Then the chief priests and elders participated in a payoff to silence the witnesses. They were instructed to say that the disciples stole His body while they slept.

After His resurrection, Jesus showed Himself alive by many infallible proofs. He appeared to Mary Magdalene and Mary, the mother of Jesus, and other women, to the eleven disciples, to the two on the Emmaus Road, and to over 500 believers (1 Cor. 15:4-7). They were convinced that He was alive—so convinced that most of them laid down their lives to share the truth of His resurrection.

His blood is efficacious to cleanse from sin, but only because He arose from the dead. The confession we must make to be saved is that Jesus is Lord (Rom. 10:9). He is above all others. He has earned this title because of what we must believe in our hearts: that God raised Him from the dead. Yes, Jesus is Lord, and He is God. His resurrection proved it.

Is the resurrection of Christ just a historical fact, or is it relevant to our lives today? It is extremely relevant. We spoke of the pain, the sting of death, but Christ removed this sting. "O Death, where is your sting? O Hades [grave], where is your victory? . . . But thanks be to God, who gives us the victory through our Lord Jesus Christ" (1 Cor. 15:55, 57).

Imagine the pain, the feeling of hopelessness when laying the body of a loved one in the grave. If we did not know that death was conquered and that we would see that person again, it would be unbearable. But praise God, you and I need never know that pain—all because Christ died for us and arose triumphantly.

HAVE YOU HEARD THE GOOD NEWS? HE'S GOT A GLORIOUS BODY FOR YOU!

My husband and I had a confession of our faith engraved on the grave marker of our precious baby. It said, "Philip! Yes, Lord!" God called; he answered. It was this reality that prevented Philip's death from crushing me, that removed the terrible pain. I know I will see him again. Not only is Philip with Jesus because of Christ's resurrection, but one day I also will be with him. Together our earthly bodies will be changed to be like Christ's glorious body.

Hallelujah for the empty tomb! His death worked together for good—your good, my good. Yes, He conquered death so that we can experience the resurrection from the dead. At that day the dead in Christ shall rise. We will have glorious bodies. "The body is sown in corruption, it is raised in incorruption. It is sown in dishonor, it is raised in glory. It is sown in weakness, it is raised in power. It is sown a natural body, it is raised a spiritual body" (1 Cor. 15:42-44).

We do not know exactly what our glorified body will be like, but we know enough. The apostle John tells us, "Beloved, now we are children of God; and it has not yet been revealed what we shall be, but we know that when He is revealed, we shall be like Him, for we shall see Him as He is" (1 John 3:2).

We also have the promise of living the resurrection life here and now. Yes, someday I shall be completely like Him, but until then I've been given the goal of growing into His likeness as I lean on Him. In my own strength I could never do this, but I have been given His resurrection power to accomplish this task. The wonderful truths in Romans 6 tell us how to live in this power.

Baptism is God's wonderful illustration of living in the likeness of His resurrection. You see, baptism illustrates two magnificent truths—one about Jesus and one about you and me.

The first truth: Going under the water in baptism illustrates Christ's death and burial; coming up out of the water illustrates His resurrection from the dead.

The second truth: Our going under the water illustrates that we are dead to our old sinful way of life. It is "buried with Christ." "Therefore we were buried with Him through baptism into death" (Rom. 6:4).

As an expression of our faith we are counting (reckoning) on the fact of His death, that He died to sin once for all (Rom. 6:10). "Likewise you also, reckon [count] yourselves to be dead indeed to sin" (Rom. 6:11a).

Coming up out of the baptismal water illustrates our "resurrection life." It is a brand-new life—that just as Christ was raised from the dead by the glory of the Father, even so we also should walk in newness of life (Rom. 6:4). We can now count ourselves "alive to God in Christ Jesus our Lord" (Rom. 6:11b).

So we are dead to sin, free from sin, free not to sin. Praise God! You can't be more relevant than that. This freedom cannot be achieved by trying to live right. It can only come through counting on the power of His death and resurrection life. His life is now coursing through our life. Count on it! Act on it! It's true! And that's good news!

HAVE YOU HEARD THE GOOD NEWS?
HE'S COMING BACK AGAIN!

The Scriptures tell us to abide or to be living in vital union with Jesus. We should abide in Him so that when He appears "we may have confidence and not be ashamed before Him at His coming" (1 John 2:28).

His return is not just an event we are wishing for. It is one of God's wonderful promises we can count on. Forty days after His resurrection Jesus led His disciples and many followers to the Mount of Olives. "While they watched, He was taken up, and a cloud received Him out of their sight. And . . . two men stood by them in white apparel, who also said, '. . . why do you stand gazing up into heaven? This same Jesus, who was taken up from you into heaven, will so come in like manner as you saw Him go into heaven'" (Acts 1:9-11).

This same Jesus is coming back again. The Bible calls it a "blessed hope." When the Bible speaks of hope, it means something I can bank on, not something I can only wish for.

Some details we don't know, but there are some exciting details we can know. One of them is that He is coming back the same way He went. That means He is coming in the clouds (Mark 13:26). There's also going to be a mighty shout, with the voice of an archangel and with the trumpet of God (1 Thess. 4:16). What a celebration it's going to be!

And it only gets better. Jesus is going to bring with Him our loved ones who have already gone on before us. The Scriptures say, "If we believe that Jesus died and rose again," we can also believe that He will bring our loved ones with Him (1 Thess. 4:14). Talk about "good news." There'll be baby Philip, my daddy, my mother, Adrian's parents, and other loved ones and friends.

Our families recently had a reunion. It was good to see many loved ones I had not seen in a long time. But some were not there because they had gone on home to be with Jesus.

One of the exciting events of our family reunion was watching movies of our families. It was neat to see Daddy and my grandmother and grandfather when they were still alive. Then I saw pictures of my husband's grandfather, whom I had never met. We all had a wonderful time reminiscing and catching up on events we had missed. It was a grand meeting! But just think of that meeting in the skies one day when we'll see Jesus—all of *us* together with all of *them*.

WILL YOU BELIEVE AND RECEIVE THE GOOD NEWS?

Now you have heard the good news. Will you believe it? Will you receive it? Don't you want to know the Good Shepherd personally? Don't you want to be a part of that meeting in the air? Don't you want to possess the magnificent assurance that "all things work together for good"—even in the darkest night?

Here is a message written by my husband, Adrian Rogers, titled "Love Worth Finding." Follow these simple steps, then sincerely pray, and you can know Jesus personally and enter into this assurance.

Psychologists have long known that every person has two great longings and inward needs. The first is to be loved, and the second is to love. But when pressures and heartaches come into our lives, many give up any hope of ever finding love. The tragedy is that we often look in the wrong places to fill this deep need and longing. Some substitute lust for love. Others pursue material things or superficial relationships—all in the futile attempt to fill a God-shaped vacuum in the human heart.

But there is good news. There is a love worth finding and a love worth sharing. The Bible says, "For God so loved the world, that he gave his only begotten Son, that whosoever believeth in him should not perish, but have everlasting life" (John 3:16 KJV).

On the cross of Christ, God's mighty love was revealed and offered unconditionally to all who would be saved. Do you long to know this mighty love? Then I need to ask you the most important question you'll ever be asked: Do you know beyond a shadow of a doubt that God loves you, that your sins are forgiven, and that you are saved and on your way to heaven? The great news is, you can know. Let me share with you how to discover the greatest love worth finding.

Admit Your Sin—First, you must admit that you are a sinner. The Bible says, "There is none righteous, no, not one" (Rom. 3:10 KJV). "For all have sinned and come short of the glory of God" (Rom. 3:23 KJV).

Abandon Your Efforts—Second, you must abandon any efforts to save yourself. If we could save ourselves, Jesus' death would have been unnecessary. "Getting religion" cannot get you to heaven. The Bible says it is "not by works of righteousness which we have done, but according to his [God's] mercy he saved us" (Titus 3:5 KJV). Salvation is by God's grace, "not of works, lest any man should boast" (Eph. 2:8-9 KJV).

Acknowledge Christ's Payment—What you cannot do for yourself, Jesus Christ has done for you. "But God demonstrates His own love toward us, in that while we were still sinners, Christ died for us" (Rom. 5:8). He died on the cross for you and then rose from the dead to prove that His payment was acceptable to God. But you must acknowledge and believe this fact. "Believe on the Lord Jesus Christ, and thou shalt be saved" (Acts 16:31 KJV).

Accept Christ as Your Savior—Salvation is God's gift to you. "The gift of God is eternal life in Jesus Christ our Lord" (Rom. 6:23b). When someone offers you a priceless gift, the wisest thing you can do is accept it. This moment you can receive Christ's gift of salvation by sincerely praying this simple prayer from your heart:

Dear God, I know I am a sinner. I know You love me and want to save me. Jesus, I believe You are the Son of God who died on the cross to pay for my sins. I believe God raised You from the dead. I now turn from my sin and, by faith, receive You as my personal Lord and Savior. Come into my heart, Lord Jesus. In Your name I pray. Amen.

Friend, if you have not yet made a decision for Christ, I urge you to receive Him today. You'll be eternally glad to know this love worth finding.

Notes

Chapter 1: Leaning on Jesus in Our Grief

1. Peter Kreeft, *Three Philosophies of Life* (Ft. Collins, Colo.: Ignatius Press, 1989), 95.
2. Ibid.

Chapter 2: "Sonlight" at Midnight

1. "Never Alone," anonymous hymn.
2. Andrew Murray, *The Believer's Secret of Waiting on God* (Minneapolis: Bethany House Publishers, 1986), 68-69.
3. Ibid., 67-68.

Chapter 3: The Problem of Unanswered Prayer

1. Henry L. Blackaby and Claude V. King, *Experiencing God* (Nashville, Tenn.: The Sunday School Board of the Southern Baptist Convention, 1990), 37.
2. Ibid.

Chapter 4: Together for Good

1. Elisabeth Elliot, *These Strange Ashes* (San Francisco: Harper and Row, 1979), 110.
2. Ibid., 111.
3. Ibid., 112.

Chapter 7: Choosing to Become Like Jesus

1. Oswald Chambers, *My Utmost for His Highest* (Grand Rapids, Mich.: Discovery House Publishers, 1935), February 10 entry.